Iraq 1941

The battles for Basra, Habbaniya, Fallujah and Baghdad

Campaign • 165

Iraq 1941

The battles for Basra, Habbaniya, Fallujah and Baghdad

Robert Lyman · Illustrated by Howard Gerrard

First published in Great Britain in 2006 by Osprey Publishing,
Midland House, West Way, Botley, Oxford OX2 0PH, UK
44-02 23rd St, Suite 219, Long Island City, NY 11101, USA
Email: info@ospreypublishing.com

Osprey Publishing is part of the Osprey Group.

Transferred to digital print on demand 2011

First published 2006
4th impression 2009

Printed and bound by Cadmus Communications, USA

A CIP catalogue record for this book is available from the British Library

ISBN: 978 1 84176 991 2

The author, Robert Lyman, has asserted his right under the Copyright,
Designs and Patents Act, 1988, to be identified as the Authors of this Work.

Design by The Black Spot
Index by Glyn Sutcliffe
Maps by The Map Studio
3D bird's-eye views by The Black Spot
Battlescene artwork by Howard Gerrard
Originated by United Graphics, Singapore

Acknowledgements
I am grateful to a wide range of people for their various kindnesses in
assisting me to complete this book. I would like to thank David Preston,
the Reverend Philip and Mrs Isla Brownless, Gordon Graham,
Gaby Kiwarkis, Sergeant Isaac Dinkha (Iraq Levies), Michael Skeet,
Dick Hennessy-Walsh, Colonel W.H. Gerard Leigh CVO OBE MC DL, His Grace
The Duke of Wellington KG LVO OBE MC DL, Dr Christopher Morris and
the members of the RAF Habbaniya Association, Peter Bindloss,
Bob Maslen-Jones, Mrs Naida Davies (nee Smart), Sergeant John Kohne
US Army, Jim Glass and Christopher Shores.

Particular thanks go to those individuals and institutions who have
provided photographs, namely the RAF Habbaniya Association, Peter
Bindloss, Jim Glass, the National Army Museum, National Archives and
the Trustees of the Imperial War Museum, London. The staff at Prince
Consort's Library Aldershot; the National Army Museum; the
Departments of Documents and Photographs at the Imperial War
Museum, the National Archives at Kew, the John Rylands Library in
Manchester, the British Library and the Household Cavalry Museum
Windsor were all unfailingly helpful. I am particularly grateful to Carol
O'Brien, my editor at Constable & Robinson, for permission to make
extensive use of material prepared for my *A Close-Run Thing: Britain and
the Struggle for Mastery in the Middle East, 1941* (Constable & Robinson,
2006). The painting by Frank Wotten of the air battle above Habbaniya
is published with kind permission of the Officers' Mess, RAF Valley.
Last, but not least, Alexander Stilwell guided the whole project
throughout with calm professionalism.

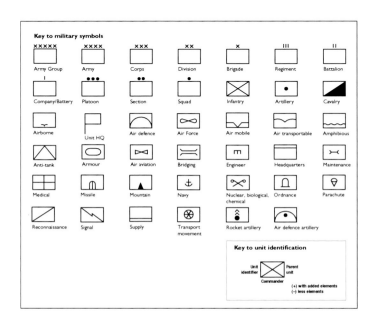

CONTENTS

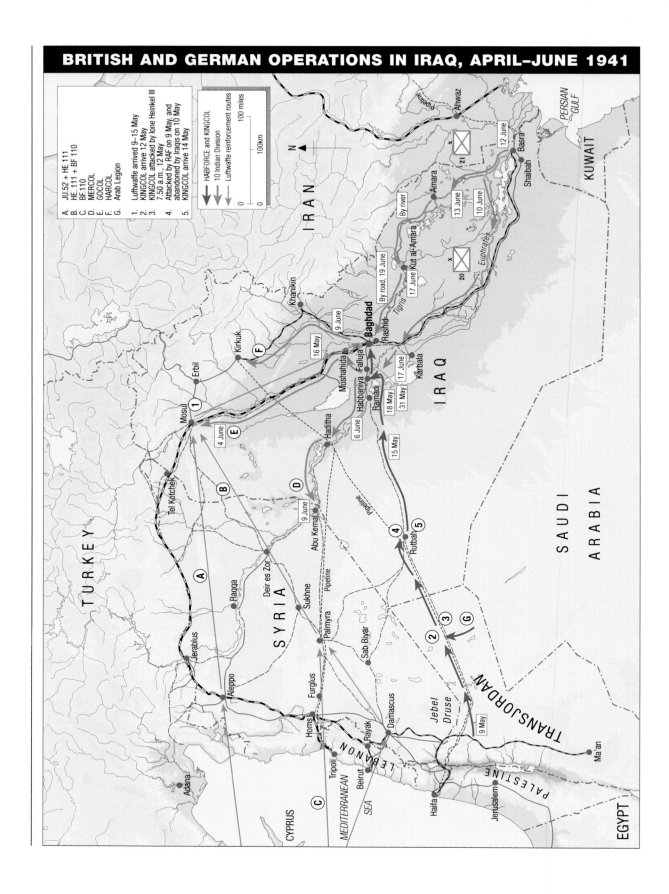

BRITISH AND GERMAN OPERATIONS IN IRAQ, APRIL–JUNE 1941

A. JU 52 + HE 111
B. HE 111 + BF 110
C. BF 110
D. MERCOL
E. GOCOL
F. HARCOL
G. Arab Legion

1. Luftwaffe arrived 9–15 May
2. KINGCOL arrive 12 May
3. KINGCOL attacked by lone Heinkel III 7.50 a.m., 12 May
4. Attacked by RAF on 9 May, and abandoned by Iraqis on 10 May
5. KINGCOL arrive 14 May

HABFORCE and KINGCOL
10 Indian Division
Luftwaffe reinforcement routes

100 miles
100km

ORIGINS OF THE CAMPAIGN

THE IMPORTANCE OF IRAQ

Iraq was very important to Great Britain in 1941 for a number of reasons. First, together with Iran, it supplied Great Britain with all of its non-American oil. But in early 1941 the continuing support of the United States, a country which was not yet committed to an active involvement in the war, was by no means certain. If all sources of oil were denied to her, Britain would no longer have the wherewithal to fight and she would have to sue for an ignominious and unimaginable peace.

In Iraq two pipelines carried oil for some 1,200 miles from Kirkuk to the Mediterranean. A single pipeline took the oil from Kirkuk to Haditha on the Euphrates, after which it bifurcated, one pipeline going through Syria to Tripoli and the other travelling south-west to the Euphrates, before turning due west and running through Transjordan to Haifa. Pumping stations were placed at intervals along each pipeline to assist in the flow of the oil. Between Kirkuk and Haditha the stations were numbered off in sequence 'K1', 'K2' and so on. After Haditha, they were numbered according to the appropriate terminus: those going to Tripoli, for instance, were numbered T1, T2 and T3, and those to Haifa H1, H2 and H3. The pumping stations were invariably manned, and formed important oases in the desert, containing a small fort, accommodation for the staff, a well and a power generator for electricity. Following the fall of France in June 1940, the British had already cut off the French

An oil pumping station, typical of the ones that dotted the pipelines from Kirkuk to Tripoli and Haifa. During the campaign these became targets for Bedouin looters and the irregulars serving under Fawzi el-Qawujki. (IWM CM818)

pipeline through Syria to Tripoli and planned to destroy the oil pipelines if Germany managed to seize control of Turkey and Syria. The principal exit point for Iranian oil was the massive refinery at Abadan, some thirty miles south-east of Basra on the Shatt al-Arab waterway.

Second, possession of Iraq's oil denied this precious commodity to Germany. Even the relatively small amount produced in the Middle East in 1940, proportionate to the dominance of US production, would have met all of Germany's petroleum needs. In 1941 Germany's only source of oil was Romania and Russia, but it was anticipated that she would need to draw on sources further afield. Indeed, the need to secure the Caucasian oil fields was to be a significant factor in Hitler's drive into Russia that summer and the denial of oil to Germany was a critical factor in Great Britain's contingency planning during 1940.

Third, the loss of Iraq would have provided a significant psychological boost to Arab nationalism elsewhere in the Middle East at the time. Iraq had been, since the late 1930s, the home of a new brand of militant Arab nationalism which sought both to thwart plans to create a Jewish homeland in Palestine and to build a new, unified Arab state from the detritus left by the collapse of the Ottoman Empire in 1918. Had Great Britain been defeated in Iraq, its hold on both Palestine and Egypt – both physical and political – would have been weakened and thus her ability to defend these strategically sensitive countries from simultaneous external and internal threats would have been much more difficult. Palestine had already suffered the Arab Revolt between 1936 and 1939, and there were plenty of nationalists in Egypt willing and prepared to rise up against the British. Because of this, the region was vulnerable to Axis propaganda and influence. The loss of Iraq, with Rommel attacking Egypt from the west, might have proved enough to eject the British from Egypt altogether, with all the implications this would have meant for the loss to the Allies of the Suez Canal.

Fourth, the loss of Iraq would threaten the security of Egypt's north-eastern flank through Turkey, Syria and Palestine. Following the collapse of France in June 1940, Syria remained under the control of a Vichy regime that was increasingly pro-German, and Turkey's neutrality would not have stood for much against a determined attack by Hitler intent on securing the Suez Canal. In late 1940 Great Britain was fearful of this possibility.

Finally, of course, the loss of Iraq would have broken the vital line of communication between the Mediterranean and India and a crucial supply route to Palestine from the east if Egypt had fallen to Rommel.

BRITISH COLONIAL RULE IN IRAQ

Iraq was mandated to Great Britain by the League of Nations in 1920. Granted independence in 1932, Iraq bound itself in 1930 through a mutual assistance agreement to Great Britain – the Anglo-Iraq Treaty – for 25 years. The primary British interest in the country was, of course, her oil. The sale of oil became a significant element of Iraq's export income, although Great Britain took a large share of the profits through the Iraq Petroleum Company (IPC). In exchange for Iraq's friendship and protection of the oil flowing towards the Mediterranean, Great Britain

The RAF Habbaniya signpost
from the Ramadi–Falluja road.
(IWM E3336)

LONDON,BAGHDAD
3287 MILES, 55 MILES

ROYAL AIR FORCE
HABBANIYA
حبانية

RAF Habbaniya from the air.
(David Jones via RAF Habbaniya
Association)

committed herself to assist in the defence of Iraq. Accordingly Great
Britain was granted the right to maintain two air bases in the country and
to recruit local levies to assist in their security. In due course, a large RAF
base was constructed at Lake Habbaniya on the Euphrates, some 55 miles
due west of Baghdad, to replace the RAF cantonment at Hinaidi, on the
outskirts of Baghdad. The long established base at Shaibah, 16 miles south
west of Basra, was retained, together with base and port facilities at Basra.
A significant topographical feature in the area between Ramadi and
Baghdad were the Euphrates 'bunds'. The Euphrates was contained for
the most part by artificial embankments that kept the water, when it rose
above the height of the surrounding plain, from spilling, but in the days
before damming it was necessary occasionally to relieve the pressure and
height of the Euphrates at Ramadi by cutting the bunds, allowing surplus
water to drain into Lake Habbaniya. Regulators controlled the flow of

The Euphrates at Habbaniya, from the escarpment. (Jim Glass)

A photograph showing the flooding around the bunds west of Baghdad in May and June 1941. Here, a section of 1 Essex is about to cross the gap in the road to Ramadi with a small boat. (IWM E3303)

water from the rivers into the canal system. If the bund had to be cut, the surrounding area would remain flooded and thus inaccessible by foot or wheel-based transport for anything between 15 and 30 days.

Habbaniya also became an important staging post on the aerial route to India and the Far East for the military transport aircraft and the flying boats of Imperial Airways, and a potential route by which Egypt could be reinforced in time of emergency. But RAF Habbaniya was almost impossible to defend. Between the base and Lake Habbaniya lay a steep escarpment leading to a wide plateau some 200 feet high, which entirely dominated the base. Immediately below the escarpment lay the airfield and the base itself, a vast camp of some 500 acres, secure behind a seven-mile-long steel fence guarded by the Levies. Blockhouses with machine-guns were sited every 300 yards or so. The rear of the base was formed by the mighty Euphrates river, in spate at this time of year.

Habbaniya was a cantonment built on the self-contained Indian model, and included everything that those stationed there, both military or civilian, might require without having to venture outside the wire. Adjacent to the airfield were the aircraft hangars for Number 4 Service Flying Training School and the Iraq Communications Flight, behind which the base was carefully and methodically laid out to reflect a little British oasis in the desert.

The relationship between Great Britain and Iraq grew more difficult as the 1930s progressed. Superficially, Iraq remained a British ally and relations between Britain and King Faisal were warm. The country was made up of a variety of competing tribes and religious groupings – Shi'ite Muslims, Sunni Muslims, Kurds, Assyrians, Bedouin Arabs, Christians and Jews, amongst others – none owing loyalty for long to anything other than their own distinct identity. The Royal family was itself an external imposition: Faisal was a Sunni Muslim, whereas most of his subjects were Shi'ites. He had substantial minorities with which to contend, none of which felt any natural affinity to him as their ruler.

The latter years of the 1930s saw nationalist sentiment grow dramatically, fed in part by the collapse of the Arab Revolt in Palestine and the escape of many of the ringleaders, including the 'Grand Mufti' of Jerusalem (Haj Amin el-Huseini), to sanctuary in Baghdad. Coups and political assassinations became a regular feature of the internal political landscape from 1932. Following Faisal's death in 1931, his 19-year-old son, Ghazi, took the Hashemite throne, but was himself killed in a car accident in 1939. At the onset of the war his pro-British uncle, Emir Abdullah, ran Iraq on behalf of Ghazi's five-year-old son, Faisal II. Because of his friendship with Great Britain, the Regent was the subject of political intrigue by extreme nationalists determined to undermine his position.

By 1941 much of the hostility towards Great Britain came from a younger generation of military officers who resented the continuing influence of Britain and the retention of power by a closed circle of elderly politicians. One influential group of officers was a cabal of four colonels in the Iraqi armed forces, nicknamed 'The Golden Square'. By 1940 these men exercised real power in Iraqi politics, successive governments depending on the support of the military for their survival. This virulently anti-British clique had long looked to Germany for support for their cause, enthusiastically encouraged since the mid 1930s by Dr Fritz Grobba, the German ambassador.

The majority view by this time amongst the Iraqi political establishment was that Britain's demise at the hands of the Axis powers was only a matter of time. Consequently, they believed that the treaty obligations with Great Britain should only be respected in the minimum way and that a neutral stance ought to be adopted towards the war. For some time the Iraqi Government had been in secret communication with both Italy and Germany, through both the Italian Consul and the Grand Mufti, and German gifts, flattery and propaganda had made substantial inroads into popular Iraqi consciousness. Meetings had been held in Ankara and Berlin between Iraqi and German politicians and diplomats, and impounded French weaponry in Syria was secretly transported to Iraq.

By early 1941 Iraqi politics were destabilizing rapidly. The new Prime Minister was a virulently anglophobic, nationalistic lawyer called Rashid Ali el Gailani, who led a government deeply divided in its attitude to Great

Britain. The Regent, pressed hard by the British and Americans, attempted in January to force Rashid Ali to resign. But the Regent's calculations misfired; the whole cabinet resigned in late January 1941 and the government was thrown into turmoil. The Regent appointed two new ministers on 28 January, a power struggle ensued and the Regent fled in fear of his life that evening, seeking safe haven with friendly tribes 100 miles south of Baghdad. Accepting the possibility of civil war in Iraq, Rashid Ali resigned and on 31 January 1941 General Taha el-Hashimi was appointed Prime Minister by the now dominant Golden Square.

Despite Rashid Ali's voluntary relinquishment of power, relations between Iraq and Great Britain failed to recover, in part because of Rashid's continued manipulation of power behind the scenes. The scale of Rashid Ali's dialogue with both Italy and Germany was by now abundantly clear to London. On 9 April a joint German and Italian statement of support was sent to Rashid Ali, promising military and financial assistance but without being specific about when this would be forthcoming. The same message – one of potential, future assistance in which Germany would *support* rather than *lead* an uprising against Britain – was repeated in a declaration that reached Iraq on 16 April 1941. Both statements led Iraqi nationalists to believe that German assistance would be instantly forthcoming in the event of war. All the signs that they would do so – German victories in the Balkans and North Africa – appeared propitious, so much so that Rashid Ali and the Golden Square were encouraged to seize power once and for all. They did so in a military *coup d'état* on 1 April 1941.

THE COMING OF WAR

The Golden Square deposed the Prime Minister, General Taha el-Hashimi, and Rashid Ali was appointed in his stead. The Regent, recognizing just in time what was about to happen, fled for protection to the American envoy, who secreted him to safety at RAF Habbaniya under a carpet in the back of his car, after which he was flown to safety at Basra and the protective hull of the elderly British river gun-boat HMS *Cockchafer*. He spent the next two months as a guest of the British in Jerusalem. In Baghdad Rashid immediately declared himself leader of a 'National Defence Government' and proceeded to arrest many leading pro-British citizens and politicians, although a good many also escaped by various means and routes, most to Amman in Transjordan.

The coup leaders' immediate plans were to refuse any further concessions to Great Britain, retain diplomatic links with Italy and expel the most prominent pro-British politicians from the country. Their aim at this stage was to exert maximum political and diplomatic pressure on Great Britain to persuade the ex-mandatory power that counter-action against Iraq would be futile, and if possible to push the British out without necessarily resorting to force. The coup was evidence of the Golden Square's conviction both that Britain was a spent force and that Germany would make good its promises of aid to Iraq in the event that a military clash became inevitable. Despite Britain's widespread interests in the country, the plotters to a man believed that, as a result of her increasing military weakness, Great Britain would attempt to negotiate with the new government, regardless of its legality.

Great Britain had not prepared militarily or politically for a *coup d'état* should it come, and British interests in Iraq plodded along complacently, seemingly oblivious to the threat facing them. On 6 April an increasingly nervous AVM Smart, Air Officer Commanding (AOC) Iraq, asked Cairo for reinforcements. Wavell and his Air Officer Commanding Middle East, Air Marshal Sir Arthur Longmore, however, believing Iraq to be a low priority compared with Greece and Libya, rejected the request. Habbaniya remained vulnerable and alone.

The respective departments of the British government and military responsible for the Middle East remained deeply divided throughout early 1941 as to the appropriate action to take with regard to the problem of Iraq. In Cairo, the C-in-C Middle East, General Sir Archibald Wavell, believed that military intervention would be a disastrous over-reaction. He was concerned that military action in Iraq might serve to inflame anti-British passions across the region, and by causing revolts and rebellions could serve to weaken yet further Britain's hold on its interests in the Middle East. Wavell's view was that Iraq was a sideshow to the main arena of war in North Africa and the Mediterranean, where he was confronted by strong enemy forces in the field, and that firm political action alone would be required.

In New Delhi, by contrast, the C-in-C India, LtGen Claude Auchinleck, and the Viceroy of India, Lord Linlithgow, strongly disagreed, urging immediate military intervention in Iraq to strengthen Britain's defences in the region. India had long been concerned about the effect instability in the rich, oil-bearing regions of Iraq and Iran would have on India's security.

Contingency plans had existed in India since August 1939 to send forces to the Persian Gulf in the event of a threat to the Iranian oil fields, the primary predator at the time being Russia. In the course of 1940 as the nature of the threat changed, particularly with the prospect of an Axis attack on Iraq through Vichy-held Syria, these plans were altered. The main plan, for three infantry divisions to be built up in Iraq, based on Basra, was called Operation *Sabine*.

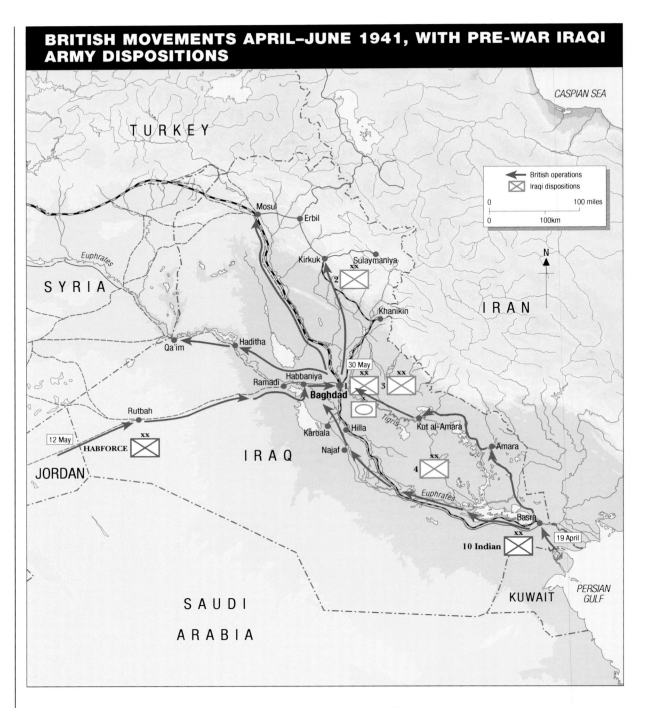

In March and April 1941, as the German war machine bore down on Yugoslavia, Egypt and Greece, the prospect of a German breach of Turkey into Syria, Iraq and Palestine became ever more a possibility. Auchinleck became increasingly fearful that the lack of robust action by Britain – both political and military – could lead to the loss of Iraq altogether, with disastrous consequences for India.

Churchill and the Chiefs of Staff agreed with Auchinleck, and insisted that Cairo took responsibility for responding to the unfolding events in

Iraq. The War Office asked Wavell on 3 April what military forces he could provide in the event that intervention in Iraq might be required. From the outset Churchill advocated the non-recognition of Rashid Ali's new National Defence Government. On 7 April Wavell replied to the effect that all he had to spare in an emergency was a single British battalion in Palestine, and that 'any other action is impossible with existing resources.' He concluded that the only alternative was for Iraq to be contained by strong diplomatic action and an aerial 'demonstration' by the RAF in Iraq. Otherwise, he could do nothing else to help.

Churchill, however, overruled him. On 4 May 1941, by which time the crisis in Iraq had boiled over into violence, Churchill ordered him to dispatch a force from Palestine to assist in the defence of British treaty rights in the country from the illegal Iraqi regime. It was the only time during the war when the Prime Minister directly overruled a Commander-in-Chief in the field. London would take full responsibility for the outcome.

CHRONOLOGY

1941

1 April *Coup d'état* in Baghdad. Prime Minister (General Taha el-Hashimi) is deposed and Regent Emir Abdullah flees to the British at RAF Habbaniya for safety and is spirited out of country in a British gunboat, HMS *Cockchafer*.
In Western Desert, Rommel captures Mersa Brega.

2 April Regent escapes to RAF Habbaniya and the new British ambassador, Sir Kinahan Cornwallis, arrives in Baghdad.

3 April War Office asks Wavell what forces he could deploy to Iraq in an emergency.
Rommel captures Benghazi.

6 April AVM Smart (AOC Iraq) asks Longmore for reinforcements, but the request is rejected.

7 April Wavell tells War Office that military intervention in Iraq is beyond his means, and counsels diplomacy.
Rommel captures Derna.

12 April Convoy BP7 sets off from Karachi for Basra with lead elements of 20 Indian Infantry Brigade.

16 April Cornwallis informs Iraqi Government that Great Britain will soon be landing forces at Basra under the terms of the Anglo-Iraq Treaty.

17 April Iraqi Government asks Germany for military assistance in event of a war with Great Britain.
364 troops of the 1 Battalion King's Own Royal Regiment land at RAF Shaibah near Basra after travelling in stages from Karachi, in the first large scale airlift of British troops in the war.

19 April First contingent of 10 Indian Division begins arriving uninvited at Maqil Docks, Basra and begins building up a base.
6 Gladiators sent from Egypt to reinforce RAF Habbaniya.

29 April Evacuation of 250 British civilians from Baghdad, and escape of others (350) to British Embassy and US Legation (150).
Iraqis mount a siege of the British air base and cantonment west of Baghdad.
1 King's Own fly from RAF Shaibah to reinforce RAF Habbaniya.
Remaining elements of 20 Indian Infantry Brigade land at Basra.

30 April Iraqi ultimatum to AVM Smart to cease operations at RAF Habbaniya.

1 May Despatch by AVM Longmore in Cairo of 18 Wellington bombers to RAF Shaibah.

2 May British pre-emptively strike hard at the besiegers at Habbaniya.
20 Indian Infantry Brigade consolidate positions west at Maqil port north of Basra.

3 May Wavell ordered by Churchill to send an expeditionary force from Palestine to relieve RAF Habbaniya.
Heavy RAF attacks on Royal Iraqi Air Force bases around Baghdad.

4 May Four Blenheim fighters arrive at RAF Habbaniya from Cairo.
Heavy RAF attacks continue on Royal Iraqi Air Force bases around Baghdad.

6 May Iraqi forces flee back to Falluja and Ramadi from the heights above RAF Habbaniya. The siege of Habbaniya lifted.
Arrival in Basra of convoy carrying land elements of 21 Indian Infantry Brigade.

8 May 10 Indian Division secure Ashar and thus whole of Basra and Shaibah area.
Wavell (C-in-C Middle East) takes command of Southern Iraq from Gen E.P. Quinan, GOC of *Force Sabine*.

11 May Habforce finally leaves Palestine en route for Iraq across 500 miles of desert.

15 May First attack by Luftwaffe (Heinkel III) on lead elements of Habforce.

18 May Kingcol arrives at Habbaniya and prepares for attack on Falluja.
MajGen Clark arrives in Habbaniya by air with the new AOC, AVM D'Albiac.

19 May Successful attack on Falluja by composite 'Habbaniya Brigade'.

22 May Strong but unsuccessful counter attack on Falluja by 6 Iraqi Infantry Brigade from the direction of Baghdad.

25 May Arrival of Habforce at Habbaniya.

27 May Northern Column leaves Falluja and crosses the Euphrates in an advance to the north of Baghdad to cut the Baghdad-Mosul road and railway.
The 10 Indian Division begins the advance north from Basra, 20 Brigade by road and 21 Brigade, in Operation *Regatta*, by boat up the Tigris.

28 May Southern Column leaves Falluja and leads advance towards Baghdad, capturing the fort at Khan Nuqta.
Failure of British attacks on Iraqi defences at Abu Ghuraib regulator.

29 May Failure of Northern Column to break through at Al Kadhimain.
Southern Column successfully crosses Abu Ghuraib canal, five miles short of Baghdad.
Rashid Ali and a group of 40, including the Grand Mufti, escape across the border to Iran.

30 May Escape of Dr Fritz Grobba, German Ambassador, from Baghdad to Mosul.

31 May Surrender of Baghdad.

1 June Return of the Regent Emir Abdullah to Baghdad.

3 June Mosul occupied by air landed troops of 2/4 Gurkha Rifles.

5 June Kirkuk occupied.

6 June Mercol engages Fawzi el-Qawujki at Abu Kemal and chases guerrillas across the Syrian border.

OPPOSING COMMANDERS

BRITISH COMMANDERS

The two most senior British commanders in the region in May 1941 were Generals **Archibald Wavell** and **Claude Auchinleck**.

General Archibald Wavell was appointed C-in-C Middle East in July. In 1940 he was widely viewed as Britain's only general and was highly regarded as a commander, being popular with the British public at a time when few British generals received any public acclaim. Wavell's greatest success in the war was against the Italians in North and East Africa in December 1940. Thereafter, things went down hill. In March he despatched 50,000 troops and 8,000 vehicles to Greece, dangerously denuding North Africa of the resources necessary to prevent Libya and Egypt being over-run by GenLt Erwin Rommel's Afrika Korps, which began arriving in Tripoli later in March. By early April Wavell was in deep trouble. The Greek adventure had failed dismally after the Germans had rapidly overwhelmed the country. The debacle of Crete then followed, and Rommel had penetrated across the Egyptian border by 11 April. With desperately weak forces, Wavell was forced to fight in the Western Desert, East Africa, Iraq and, in June, Syria as well. Wavell was sacked from the Middle East on 22 June 1941 and became the C-in-C India after Auchinleck. **Air Marshal Sir Arthur Longmore** was Air Officer Commanding (AOC) Middle East until early May after which he was replaced by his deputy, **Air Marshal Tedder** .

General Claude Auchinleck was commissioned into the Indian Army. In early 1941 he was appointed C-in-C India, following spells as General Officer C-in-C Northern Norway and General Officer Commanding Southern Command in England. Known as the 'Auk' he was one of the outstanding British generals of the war. In late June 1941, he swapped places with Wavell, becoming C-in-C Middle East. A series of battlefield failures in the Western Desert in 1942, however, accompanied by an increasingly bitter rift with the Prime Minister, resulted in his replacement in August 1942 by Gen Bernard Montgomery. He returned to his old post as C-in-C India and Wavell was elevated to the position of Viceroy of India.

The British ambassador from 2 April 1941 was **Sir Kinahan Cornwallis,** an old Iraq hand who had spent 20 years in the country as adviser to the now dead King Faisal. He was a highly regarded diplomat who was despatched to Iraq to hold a more forceful political line with the Iraqi Government than had hitherto been the case. He arrived too late, however, to prevent the onset of war.

The AOC Iraq, based at RAF Habbaniya, was **Air Vice-Marshal H.G. ('Reggie') Smart**. He was appointed AOC Iraq in November 1939. Slow, conservative and conventional he was unprepared mentally for the pace

Gen Sir Archibald Wavell, C-in-C Middle East. He vehemently opposed intervention in Iraq, and had to be over-ruled by Churchill. (IWM E451)

AVM Tedder, Air Officer-in-Chief Middle East. (IWM CM881)

TOP LEFT **LtGen Claude Auchinleck. As Commander-in-Chief India, the 'Auk', was a critic of Wavell's Middle Eastern policy and a firm proponent of strong military intervention in Iraq. On this occasion, Churchill entirely agreed with him. (IWM E3229E)**

TOP CENTRE **Sir Kinahan Cornwallis and MajGen J.G.W. (George) Clark, at the British Embassy, Baghdad on the day after the armistice was signed and the Embassy relieved by a column of troops, 1 June 1941. (IWM E3460)**

TOP RIGHT **LtGen 'Jumbo' Wilson, the man tasked by Wavell with making Churchill's bricks without straw, and to advance 500 miles across the desert to relieve RAF Habbaniya and seize Baghdad. (IWM E3105E)**

BELOW LEFT **Brig Joe Kingstone (centre) and MajGen G.G. Waterhouse, the head of the British Military Mission to Iraq (left). (IWM E3445)**

BELOW RIGHT **AVM Smart, Air Officer Commanding, Iraq, until 5 May, when he was evacuated, injured after a road accident, to Basra. (IWM CH14575)**

and fury of modern war. An unfortunate car accident in the dark (due to the blackout) led to his evacuation, with his family, on 5 May, first to Basra and then to India. **Colonel Ouvry Roberts**, the Chief Staff Officer to 10th Indian Division, assumed command of land operations at RAF Habbaniya, air tasking carried out by **Wing Commander Casey**. A Royal Engineer, Roberts would go on to command 23 Indian Division in the 14 Army at the battle of Imphal.

General Sir Henry Maitland ('Jumbo') Wilson, newly returned from the debacle in Greece, was made responsible on 3 May for preparing the plan to send a force overland to Iraq. The GOC of the 1 Cavalry Division, based in Palestine and on which 'Habforce' base was constructed, was **Major-General J.G.W. (George) Clark** and that of the 4th Cavalry Brigade ('Kingcol') was **Brigadier J.J. (Joe) Kingstone** late of the Queens Bays. Clark arrived at RAF Habbaniya by air on 18 May 1941, in advance of his troops, together with the new Air Officer Commanding (AOC), **Air Vice-Marshal John D'Albiac**, who had been the AOC during the campaign in Greece. The political adviser to Habforce was **Major John Bagot Glubb** ('Glubb Pasha') of the Arab Legion.

The commander of *Force Sabine* (thereafter 'Iraq Force' until 21 June, and 'Iraq Command' after that) was **Lieutenant-General Edward Quinan** of the Indian Army. The major component of *Force Sabine* during the period was the 10 Indian Division, commanded initially by **Major-General W.A.K. (William) Fraser**. However, following a loss of confidence among his staff about his leadership Fraser was removed and Quinan's Brigadier-

General Staff (BGS), **Brigadier W.J. (Bill) Slim** promoted to Major-General and given command of the division on 15 May 1941. 'Uncle Bill' Slim was one of the most dynamic and innovative British commanders of the war, loved by his soldiers in a way unknown since the days of Marlborough, Wellington and Nelson. Given command of the 14 Army in

India in late 1943, Slim took it to defeat the Japanese first at Imphal and Kohima (India) in 1944, and thence into Burma proper in 1945, defeating the Japanese in an extraordinary succession of brilliant engagements which placed him as one of the all-time great British battlefield commanders in history. General Fraser became the Military Attaché to the British Embassy in Tehran.

IRAQI COMMANDERS

The Prime Minister of the illegal Iraqi regime was an ex-lawyer and Anglophobe called **Rashid Ali el-Gailani**. The Grand Mufti of Jerusalem, **Haj Amin el-Huseini**, who escaped to Baghdad following the end of the Arab Revolt in 1939, gave him ideological, religious and political support. Haj Amin el-Huseini was virulently anti-British and anti-Jewish, and a strong supporter of Hitler and Nazism. After fleeing the end of the war in Iraq he made his home in Germany. There, he travelled extensively throughout Axis-held territory. In the Balkans he recruited Bosnian Muslims into the SS, and was implicated in the murder of thousands of Jews. A close descendant of his was the late Yasser Arafat. The power behind the regime was the so-called 'Golden Square', a cabal of armed forces officers comprising **Colonel Salah ed-Din es-Sabbagh** (Commander of the 3 Infantry Division), **Colonel Kamal Shahib** (Commander of the 1 Infantry Division), **Colonel Fahmi Said** (Commander of the Independent Mechanized Brigade) and the Air Force chief, **Colonel Mahmud Salman**. The German Ambassador, **Dr Fritz Grobba**, played a significant role over several years in wooing Iraqi policy-makers away from support for Great Britain and into Germany's embrace.

A significant thorn in the British side was the guerrilla leader **Fawzi el-Qawujki**. He served in the French-Syrian Army in the 1920s and received formal military training at the French military academy at St Cyr but deserted to join the Druze rebellion in 1925–27. He was a ruthless fighter who did not hesitate to murder or mutilate his prisoners. He remained an outlaw thereafter but was pardoned by Vichy France in 1941 if he agreed to fight against Great Britain. He did so until being wounded on 24 June 1941, when German aircraft evacuated him to Athens. After the war he led the Palestinian Liberation Army in the war of 1947, in which Glubb Pasha fought on his side. He is described in Colonel Humphrey Wyndham's history of the Household Cavalry Regiment as 'a very fine guerrilla leader and a very formidable opponent.'

Haj Amin el-Huseini, the exiled so-called 'Grand Mufti of Jerusalem' and primary nationalist demagogue for the rebel cause in Iraq.

OPPOSING FORCES

BRITISH FORCES

RAF Habbaniya
4th Service Flying Training School

A variety of aircraft were found at Habbaniya although not all could be used for offensive operations and none could be described as modern. Likewise, many of the 84 airframes on the base could not be flown or used offensively, and at the start of the battle the station boasted only 39 pilots. The inventory comprised a mixed assortment of obsolete and obsolescent bombers, fighters and trainers.

3 old Gladiator biplane fighters, used as officers' runabouts
6 Gladiator biplanes which arrived from Egypt on 19 April 1941
30 Hawker Audaxes, which could carry eight 20lb bombs. Twelve Audaxes were adjusted so that they could each carry 2 x 250lb bombs
7 Fairey Gordon biplane bombers, each of which could carry 2 x 250lb bombs
27 twin-engined Oxfords, each converted from carrying smoke bombs only to carry 160lbs of 20lb bombs
25 Hawker Harts – the bombing version of the Hawker Audax – which could carry two 250lb bombs
24 Hart-trainers, with no weaponry
1 Blenheim Mk 1 (leaving for good on 3 May)
4 Blenheim Mk IVs of 203 Squadron RAF (from Sunday 4 May)

RAF Iraq Communications Flight
3 Vickers Valentia bombers

Number 1 Armoured Car Company RAF
18 Rolls Royce Armoured Cars
2 ancient tanks, named 'Walrus' and 'Seal'

Iraq Levies

The RAF had played an important role in imperial policing in Iraq since October 1922, when it was decided, for reasons of economy, to ensure order in the newly mandated territory, not by a large and expensive standing army, but by aircraft, supported on the ground by armoured cars and backed up by locally recruited levies.

In 1941 the Iraq Levies formed by far the largest land force element at RAF Habbaniya, in six companies. These were HQ Wing, Composite Company, 1,2,3 and 4 Assyrian Companies and 8 Kurdish Company. Each company had 125 infantrymen (although the Composite Company had more), a machine-gun section, a 3-in mortar section and one anti-tank Rifle. At the start of the campaign troop numbers were 1,199, as follows:

An Audax over the Jebel Orwell. The Hawker Audax was designed for close support and Army co-operation duty at home and abroad, and first entered RAF service in 1932. By the time production ceased, 718 aircraft had been built. A single-engined, single-bay, all-metal biplane, it had one fixed, synchronized forward-firing .303 Vickers machine gun, one ring-mounted Lewis 0.303 gun in the rear cockpit, and could carry 4 x 20lb practice bombs. Its maximum speed was 170mph at 2,400 feet. Only in the Middle East and East Africa did the Audax see action, most notably in Iraq in May 1941. (IWM CH8725)

Recruits for the Iraq Levies, RAF Habbaniya, 12 May 1942. (IWM E11584)

17 British officers
5 British non-commissioned officers (NCOs)
3 Surgeons
40 Assyrian officers
1,134 Assyrian other ranks (privates and non-commissioned officers)

The levies and their families, together with civilian workers (Assyrians, Armenians, Indians and a host of other nationalities, many of whom were displaced persons following the First World War), brought the population of the cantonment in the spring of 1941 to some 9,000 souls.

RAF Shaibah
No. 244 Bomber Squadron RAF (Vincents)
No. 31 Transport Squadron RAF from 17 April (Valentias, DC-2s and Atlantas)
No. 814 Squadron Royal Naval Air Service from HMS *Hermes* (Fairey Swordfish)
No. 37 Squadron RAF (Wellingtons) from 1 to 12 May
No. 70 Squadron RAF (Wellingtons) from 1 to 12 May

H4, Transjordan
No. 84 Squadron RAF (detachment), flying five Blenheim IVs
No. 203 Squadron RAF (detachment), flying two Blenheim IVFs

Force Sabine at 15 May 1941
10 Indian Division (MajGen W.A.K. Fraser until 15 May 1941, thereafter MajGen W.J. Slim) comprising:

HQ and Signals 10 Indian Division
3 Field Regiment Royal Artillery
HQ 20 Indian Brigade arrived on Convoy BP7 on 19 April
    3/11 Sikh Regiment
    2/7 Gurkha Rifles
    2/8 Gurkha Rifles
Ancillary troops, including 26 Field Ambulance
1 Battalion King's Own Royal Regiment
    364 troops
    12l Light machine-guns
    6 Vickers heavy machine-guns
    2 anti-tank rifles

By the end of April 1941 the Royal Navy presence in the northern Persian Gulf amounted to seven ships:

HMS *Seabelle*
HMAS *Yarra*
HMS *Falmouth*
HMS *Cockchafer*
HMS *Emerald*
HMIS *Lawrence*
HMS *Hermes*

21 Indian Infantry Brigade arrived at Basra in three transports (Convoy BP1) on 6 May 1941, comprising:

4/13 Frontier Force Rifles
2/4 Gurkha Rifles
2/10 Gurkha Rifles

25 Indian Infantry Brigade arrived at Basra at the end of May 1941. This comprised:

3 Jat Regiment
2 Royal Sikh Regiment
1 Mahratta Light Infantry

Dispositions of Iraq Force as at 20 June 1941

Northern Iraq (HQ 20 Indian Brigade)

Mosul	1 King's Own Royal Regiment
	2/4 Gurkha Rifles
	Battery (less one troop) 3 Field Regiment Royal Artillery
Kirkuk	10 Field Company Royal Engineers
	2/7 Gurkha Rifles
Haditha	1 Section sappers and miners
	One Company 3/11 Sikh Regiment
	One Troop 3 Field Regiment Royal Artillery
	One troop 13 Lancers

Baghdad Area (HQ 10 Indian Division and HQ 21 Indian Brigade)

Baghdad	4/13 Frontier Force Rifles
	2/8 Gurkha Rifles (less one company)
	3/11 Sikhs (less two companies)
	3 Field Regiment Royal Artillery (less one battery)
	157 Field Regiment Royal Artillery
	One anti-tank battery
	One squadron 13 Lancers (less one troop)
	One field park company
Falluja	One company 2/8 Gurkha Rifles

Lower Iraq

Basra	17 Indian Infantry Brigade
Ur, Samawa and Diwaniya	24 Indian Infantry Brigade (less one battalion)
	13 Lancers (less one squadron)
	32 Field Regiment Royal Artillery
	19 Medium Battery, Royal Artillery
En route to Baghdad by rail	2/10 Gurkha Rifles
	25 Indian Infantry Brigade

Habforce

Based on 1 Cavalry Division, stationed in the Rehovot area in Palestine, and commanded by MajGen J.G.W (George) Clark. The division was horsed until it was 'mechanized' by giving it wheeled transport in March 1941. It was responsible for internal security in Palestine, but was directed on 3 May to be prepared to meet the new threat in Iraq. There was no talk of an advance on Baghdad until the following week, when on 8 May Habforce was formed.

HQ and Signals Regiment 1st Cavalry Division
HQ 4 Cavalry Brigade (Brig J.J. Kingstone)
  The Household Cavalry Regiment (The Life Guards and Royal Horse Guards 'Blues')
  The Royal Wiltshire Yeomanry (less one squadron)
  The Warwickshire Yeomanry (less one squadron)

1 Battalion The Essex Regiment
237 Battery of 60 Field Artillery Regiment (25-pounder guns) (less one troop)
A mechanized squadron of the Transjordan Frontier Force (TJFF)
169 Light Anti-Aircraft Battery, Royal Artillery
No. 2 Armoured Car Company RAF (8 Fordson armoured cars)
No. 1 AT (Anti-Tank) troop of the Royal Artillery (2-pdr guns)
A troop of the 2 'Cheshire' Field Squadron Royal Engineers
A detachment of 166 Light Field Ambulance.
3 Reserve Motor Transport Company, Royal Army Service Corps
552 Transport Company, Royal Army Service Corps (between them of which they had 296 3-ton and 52 30cwt supply trucks).

An advanced striking column of 2,000 men under the command of Brigadier Kingstone comprised:

HQ 4 Cavalry Brigade
Signal Troop, Middlesex Yeomanry
Light Aid Detachment (for mechanical repairs)
Household Cavalry Regiment
A and D companies, 1 Battalion Essex Regiment
237 Battery, 60 Field Regiment Royal Artillery
No. 1 AT (anti-tank) troop of the Royal Artillery (2-pdr guns)
Detachment 166 Light Field Ambulance
552 Transport Company, Royal Army Service Corps
No. 2 Armoured Car Company RAF

IRAQI FORCES

Before the war Britain provided support and training to the nascent Iraqi Army and Royal Iraqi Air Force (RIAF) through a small military mission based in Baghdad, commanded in 1941 by MajGen G.G. Waterhouse. The Iraqi army consisted of four divisions with some 60,000 troops. These were:

Army

1 Infantry Division, HQ in Baghdad (Col Kamal Shahib)
  1 Infantry brigade, Mussaiyib (40 miles south of Baghdad)
  2 Infantry brigade, Baghdad
  Field artillery brigade, Baghdad
  Mountain artillery brigade, Diwaniya (two batteries of 3.7-in howitzers attached to 4 Infantry Division)
  Divisional cavalry squadron, Jaloula (80 miles north-east of Baghdad)

2 Infantry Division, HQ in Kirkuk
  3 Infantry brigade, Mosul
  4 Infantry brigade, Kirkuk
  5 Infantry brigade, (less one battalion at Erbil)
  Field artillery brigade, Kirkuk
  Field artillery brigade, Kirkuk
  Mountain artillery brigade, Mosul
  Divisional cavalry squadron, Kirkuk

3 Infantry Division, Baghdad (Col Salah ed-Din es-Sabbagh)
  6 Infantry brigade, Baghdad
  7 Infantry brigade, Jaloula
  8 Infantry brigade, Masourat al Jebel
  Field artillery brigade

Field artillery brigade
Mountain artillery brigade
Divisional cavalry squadron, Jaloula

4 Infantry Division, Diwaniya
   Infantry brigade, Diwaniya
   Infantry brigade (2nd Line), Basra (one battalion at Amara)
   Infantry brigade (2nd Line), Nasiriya (less one battalion at Samawa)
   Mountain artillery battery, Amara (2.75-in guns)
   (Plus mountain artillery brigade of 1 Infantry Division)

Independent Mechanized Brigade, Baghdad (Col Fahmi Said)

Light Tank Company (Fiat light tanks)
Armoured Car Company (14 British-built Crossley armoured cars)
Mechanized (i.e. lorried) infantry battalion
Mechanized (i.e. lorried) infantry battalion
Mechanized machine-gun company
Mechanized artillery brigade

Each Iraqi Infantry Brigade had three Infantry Battalions, each of which at full strength had:

26 Officers and 820 other ranks
154 animals
46 Bren light machine guns
8 Vickers heavy machine-guns (in two platoons of 4 MGs each)
4 anti-aircraft Lewis guns

Royal Iraq Air Force

Squadron	Total	Purpose	Type	Location
No. 1	9	Army Co-operation	Hawker Nisr (an Audax with a Pegasus engine)	Mosul
No. 2	7	General Purpose	Vincent, Dragon, Dragonfly	Mosul
No. 4	7	Fighter	Gladiator	Rashid
No. 5	4	Fighter Bomber	Breda 65	Rashid
No. 6	4	Medium Bomber	Savoia 79	Rashid
No. 7	5	Fighter Bomber	Northrop 8A	Rashid
Flying Training School	12	Training	Tiger Moth	Rashid

An Italian Breda 65. The RIAF had four of these aircraft in service in 1941. (IWM HU2206)

The RIAF boasted a total of 116 aircraft, although only about 57 were reported to be in a serviceable condition in early 1941, most of which were based at Rashid airfield (previously known as RAF Hinaidi before it was handed over to the RIAF) in Baghdad. In addition to these figures above the RIAF had 9 Audax fighters in general use not allocated to specific squadrons, and a further 19 aircraft available in reserve, of which 4 were Breda 65 and 5 were Northrop 8A Fighter Bombers.

Navy

    4 x 100-ton Thorneycroft gunboats each armed with
      3.7-in howitzer
      3-in mortar
      4 machine-guns

    1 x pilot vessel (*King Faisal 1*) with a 4-in gun
    1 x minesweeper (*Alarm*) with a 12-pdr gun.

All were based in the Shatt-al-Arab waterway.

An Italian Savoia 79 tri-engine bomber. This aircraft was photographed in Abyssinia on 9 May 1941, at the height of the air war for Iraq. (IWM E2947)

Comparison of aircraft employed during the Iraq War [1]

Aircraft	Type	Crew	Load	Armament	Range and Speed
British					
Gladiator (fighter)	Single-engine biplane	1	Nil	4 x .303 machine-guns	245 mph at 15,000 feet
Audax (fighter)	Single-engine biplane	2	80lb	2 x .303 machine-guns	168 mph at 5,000 feet
Blenheim Mark 1 (fighter bomber)	Twin-engine monoplane	3	1,000lb	2 x .303 machine-guns	265 mph at 15,000 feet
Bombay (transport)	Twin-engine monoplane	4	24 troops or 2,000lb	2 x .303 machine-guns	159 mph at 10,000 feet
Gordon (bomber)	Single-engine biplane	2	500lb	2 x .303 machine-guns	137 mph at 5,000 feet
Oxford (trainer)	Twin-engine monoplane	3	160lb	2 x .303 machine-guns	190 mph at 10,000 feet
Valentia (bomber/transport)	Twin-engine biplane	2	22 troops or bombs	Door mounted machine-guns	111 mph at 6,500 feet
Vincent (bomber)	Single-engine biplane	2	500lb	2 x .303 machine-guns	141 mph at 10,000 feet
Wellington Mark 1 (bomber)	Twin-engine monoplane	6	4,500lb	6 x .303 machine-guns	247 mph at 17,000 feet
Italian					
CR42 (fighter)	Single-engine biplane				
Iraqi					
Gladiator (fighter)	Single-engine biplane	1	Nil	4 x .303 machine-guns	245 mph at 15,000 feet
Audax (fighter)	Single-engine biplane	2	80lb	2 x .303 machine-guns	168 mph at 5,000 feet
Breda 65 (fighter)	Single-engine monoplane	1 or 2	80lb	2 x .303 machine-guns	168 mph at 5,000 feet
Dragon (transport)	Twin-engine biplane	1	Nil	Nil	128 mph at sea level
Dragonfly (transport)	Twin-engine biplane	1	Nil	Nil	147 mph at sea level
Tiger Moth (trainer)	Single-engine biplane	2	Nil	Nil	110 mph at sea level
Northrop 8A (fighter bomber)	Single-engine monoplane	2	1,800lb	5 x .30 machine-guns	255 mph at 9,000 feet
Saviao 79 (bomber)	Three engine monoplane	5	2,750lb	2 x .303 machine-guns	141 mph at 10,000 feet
Vincent bomber	Single engine biplane	2	500lb	2 x .303 machine-guns	141 mph at 10,000 feet
German					
Bf 110 (fighter)	Twin-engine monoplane	2	Nil	6 x 7.9mm machine-guns 2 x 20mm cannon	360 mph at 20,000 feet
He 111 (bomber)	Twin-engine monoplane	6	2,200lb	6 x 7.9mm machine-guns 2 x 20mm cannon	295 mph at 14,000 feet
Ju 52	Three-engine monoplane	4	5,000lb freight	5 x 7.9mm machine-guns	165 mph at sea level

1 Source: MajGen I.S.O. Playfair

THE SEIZURE OF BASRA

On 8 April 1941, the day British troops first came into contact with Germans in Crete, Churchill asked India for troops to be sent to the defence of Basra. The Secretary of State (Amery), the Viceroy (Lord Linlithgow) and Auchinleck immediately agreed. Auchinleck signalled London on 10 April, explaining that he intended to send to Basra an infantry brigade and a field regiment of artillery, which at that moment was preparing to set sail from Karachi for Malaya. In command was MajGen William Fraser, General Officer Commanding 10 Indian Infantry Division. At the same time Churchill also ordered Wavell to despatch a 'sizeable force' from Palestine to strengthen the defence of RAF Habbaniya.

Fraser's convoy (BP7) set off from Karachi on 12 April, with the following orders:

1. To occupy the Basra–Shaibah area in order to ensure the safe disembarkation of further reinforcements and to enable a base to be established in that area.
2. In view of the uncertain attitude of the Iraqi Army and local authorities, to face the possibility that attempts might be made to oppose the disembarkation of his force.
3. Should the embarkation be opposed, to overcome the enemy by force and occupy suitable defensive positions ashore as quickly as possible.
4. To take the greatest care not to infringe the neutrality of Iran.

Britain's military strength in the region was weak. The garrison at Habbaniya was not designed to have an offensive capability and the Royal Navy had only a limited presence in the Persian Gulf, boasting four small warships at the start of April, increasing to seven as the month progressed, including the cruiser HMS *Emerald* and the carrier HMS *Hermes*, carrying the Fairey Swordfish torpedo bombers of 814 Squadron. The new Iraqi regime acted swiftly to limit the effectiveness of these forces, weak as they were. On 6 April British military personnel were prevented from travelling between Habbaniya and Baghdad and the British Military Mission was stripped of its radio transmitters.

Britain was eavesdropping on the communications between the Italian Legation in Baghdad and Rome. On 8 April the German Foreign Office issued what Rashid came to regard as a letter guaranteeing German support for any anti-British action he undertook 'as far as possible in case of any war undertaken by the Arabs against the British for their freedom.' On 17 April Rashid Ali asked for Axis assistance, particularly in the area of air support. A week later on 23 April he went further and asked not merely for weapons but for active intervention by German forces in the event of a war with Great Britain. It seems clear that Rashid Ali was planning military action against the British at least a week before it occurred, and that the landings in Basra served to unnerve him into acting precipitately.

As it was, the government of Rashid Ali was taken entirely by surprise by Britain's announcement, on 16 April, that under the terms of the Anglo-Iraq Treaty Great Britain would shortly be landing troops at Basra. On the following day the first of 364 officers and men of the 1 Battalion King's Own Royal Regiment landed in Shaibah following a four-day journey from Karachi that had taken them via Sharjah Fort in Trucial Oman and Bahrain in what was the first ever strategic airlift by British forces in war. They travelled in five high-wing Armstrong Whitworth Atlantas lent to the RAF for the operation, together with their pilots, by Imperial Airways, as well as 12 obsolescent Vickers Valentia biplane transports. Later in April, 31 Squadron was re-equipped with the new American Douglas DC2, and the 1,300-mile flight from Karachi was conducted in the much shorter period of thirteen hours. Col Ouvry Roberts, Quinan's chief staff officer in 10 Indian Division (the General Staff Officer Grade 1, or 'GSO 1'), travelled with the men of the King's Own as part of the divisional reconnaissance party. The troops of the King's Own were then flown north-west on 29 April to reinforce Habbaniya. They expected to remain in Iraq for about six weeks.

At the time of these landings the prevailing opinion in London was that they would serve forcefully to keep the lid on any potential Iraqi uprising and were principally a deterrent.

The first sea-borne convoy contained Brig D. Powell's 20 Indian Infantry Brigade. On 15 April he made his plan for the landings at Basra on the basis that it would be opposed. He assumed that the Iraqis would be disposed as follows:

300 infantry guarding the entrance to the Shatt-al-Arab at Fao
Two infantry battalions at Zubair
One infantry battalion at Tanuma
Two infantry battalions at Zubeila

Powell considered three options:

Option 1 – To land at Kuwait and move north to Basra by land. This would reduce the difficulties associated with an opposed landing but it would also involve a march of 112 miles with little water en route, giving the Iraqis at Basra plenty of advance warning of British intentions. The subsequent line of communication would also be vulnerable to guerrilla action.

Option 2 – To land at the entrance of the Shatt al-Arab at Fao. The route from Fao to Basra, however, was hindered by many water channels which would slow the advance and might easily be used by the Iraqis to oppose the advance.

Option 3 – The boldest, a *coup de main* directly up the Shatt-al-Arab to the dock area. This made best use of surprise and could carry the deception that the landing was harmless and merely in support of Britain's treaty rights. However, the eight-ship convoy was not packed to enable it to deploy immediately into action.

Powell decided on Option 3 and issued his orders on 16 April:

1. A detachment of 2/7 Gurkha would land by lifeboat at Fao and

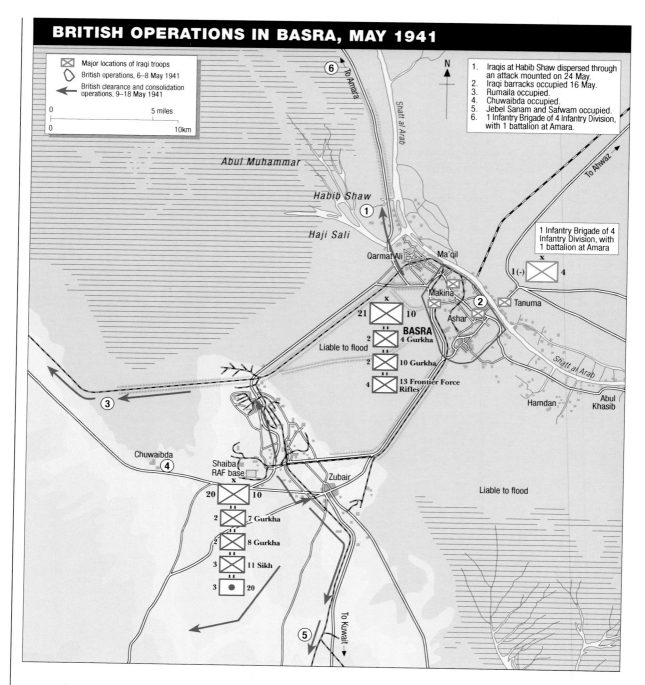

BRITISH OPERATIONS IN BASRA, MAY 1941

Major locations of Iraqi troops

British operations, 6–8 May 1941

British clearance and consolidation operations, 9–18 May 1941

0   5 miles

0   10km

N

1. Iraqis at Habib Shaw dispersed through an attack mounted on 24 May.
2. Iraqi barracks occupied 16 May.
3. Rumaila occupied.
4. Chuwaibda occupied.
5. Jebel Sanam and Safwam occupied.
6. 1 Infantry Brigade of 4 Infantry Division, with 1 battalion at Amara.

To Amara

Shatt al Arab

To Ahwaz

Abul Muhammar

Habib Shaw
1

Haji Sali

Qarmat Ali   Ma'qil

1 Infantry Brigade of 4 Infantry Division, with 1 battalion at Amara

1 (-)   4

Makina
2   Tanuma

21   10

2   4 Gurkha   BASRA

Ashar

Liable to flood

2   10 Gurkha

4   13 Frontier Force Rifles

Shatt al Arab

Hamdan   Abul Khasib

3

Chuwaibda
4

Shaiba RAF base

Zubair

Liable to flood

20   10

2   7 Gurkha

2   8 Gurkha

3   11 Sikh

3   20

To Kuwait

5

disarm the garrison, and re-embark for Basra, joining 2/8 Gurkha at the main dock area at Maqil.

2. 200 men of 2/8 Gurkha would land at the dock area at Maqil and secure the area of the RAF cantonment. The rest of the battalion would follow later to secure the whole dock area.

3. 3/11 Sikh would remain in reserve.

All battalions to be self-sufficient in food and water for 48 hours.
3 Field Regiment RA did not have access to its guns due to the fact that

the convoy had not been loaded for action on landing. Instead, it was planned to send Forward Observation Officers with the infantry battalions to act as observers for naval gunfire support. 26 Field Ambulance would open an Advanced Dressing Station at Maqil docks.

In the event, the landings on 19 April were unopposed. Two hundred men of the 2/7 Gurkha Rifles secured the dock area that day, allowing the remainder of the force to disembark on the 19th. It was fortunate for Powell's troops that the landing was unopposed, as the brigade was only partly trained and poorly equipped, and had no integral transport. The local atmosphere was nevertheless sullen and un-cooperative. The dock labourers went on strike, forcing soldiers to unload their own ships before labourers could be brought in from India.

2/8 Gurkhas took control of RAF Quay, the RAF hospital, wireless station, Maqil civil airfield and the Maqil quays with no opposition. Unnerved, Rashid Ali reacted immediately by notifying Cornwallis that, whilst the treaty permitted the arrival of the troops, the Iraqi Government insisted that the troops transit quickly through Iraq to Palestine, and that they did so in small contingents. He was obviously rattled, having on 16 April received the letter from Berlin assuring him of German support in the event of war with Britain. Not for a moment did he believe that Britain had the will or the wherewithal to fight a war in Iraq.

India was determined to follow up this landing with another convoy in early May, to bring 10 Indian Division up to strength. London, after some consideration of the options available, decided on 23 April that the 20 Brigade landing would be reinforced to divisional size and that Basra would be developed further to a state that it would be able to receive the full complement of forces (three divisions) planned for Operation *Sabine*. Other elements of 20 Brigade landed at Basra in the three ships of Convoy BP1 without incident on 29 April, despite Iraq's refusal of permission for it to land. The Iraqis decided not to oppose the landings at Basra but rather to carry out troop dispositions designed to threaten RAF Habbaniya instead.

With the onset of hostilities at Habbaniya, on 2 May Powell sought to consolidate his position around Maqil, and leave the seizure of Ashar until the 21 Indian Brigade (4/13 Frontier Force Rifles, 2/4 Gurkha Rifles and 2/10 Gurkha Rifles) arrived by ship on 6 May. Accordingly 2/8 Gurkha was despatched to guard the RAF airfield at Shaibah, 2/7 Gurkha was held in reserve and 3/11 Sikh secured the Maqil docks. Although the Iraqi army made no formal attempt to oppose the British at either Maqil or Shaibah, considerable hostility was encountered from the crowds, small groups of soldiers and from the police. Over the next couple of days sporadic violence was encountered. At 2 p.m. on 2 May the guns of 3 Regiment RA, firing from their base at Makina, dispersed a hostile mob moving from the barracks at Zubeila towards Maqil Camp. An hour-and-a-half later a group of some 50 policemen, described as 'truculent', were forcibly disarmed at the Maqil railway station by troops of 2/7 Gurkha accompanied by three armoured cars, and shortly after 4 p.m. three Vincents of 244 Squadron, sent to bomb a group of Iraqis at the Quramat Ali creek crossing, were attacked by ground fire, with the result that one aircraft was shot down. 3/11 Sikh captured an armoured train in the early evening, and further groups of policemen had to be disarmed in the area of the docks in an operation that went on well into the darkness. However, by nightfall the Maqil and Shaibah areas had been quietened, but Ashar remained a problem about which nothing could be done until 21 Indian Brigade arrived on 6 May. Until their arrival, the only offensive activity that could be undertaken was that by the Fairey Swordfish of 814 Squadron, six of which flew a demonstration flight over Basra on 3 May. On the following day four aircraft, flying off HMS *Hermes*, attacked a bridge over the Euphrates. Commanded by Brigadier C.J. Weld, the arrival of 21 Indian Brigade would double the size of the force at Basra. Fortunately, the convoy included two troops of the 13 Lancers with Indian 1922-type Rolls Royce armoured cars and a detachment of Indian Army engineers. Weld's brigade was relieved that they did not have to conduct an opposed landing, as their ships, like those of 20 Indian Brigade, had been packed in advance for an administrative rather than an operational move to Malaya. Vital equipment was scattered across the holds of a variety of ships and needed first to be married up with its owners before it could be pressed into action.

When, on 6 May, 21 Indian Brigade duly landed at the Maqil docks, it immediately provided one of its battalions, 2/4 Gurkha, to Powell to support a planned operation by 2/7 Gurkha and a half section of armoured cars from the 13 Lancers to secure the township of Ashar the following day. 2/4 Gurkha was to wait at the northern approaches to the town ready to support 2/7 Gurkha if required. The operation began at 2 a.m. on the morning of 7 May. The aim was to occupy the Iraqi naval and military headquarters in the town, as well as the police barracks, the government offices, the post, telegraph and telephone exchange offices and the banks, and to disarm the police. The battalion divided itself into two parts for the operation. Battalion Headquarters, HQ Company and B and C Companies were to move against Ashar via the river, securing the wharf. B Company was to secure a safe bridgehead to allow C Company to advance to secure the banks, post and telegraph offices. At the same time a column comprising A and D Companies, together with the three armoured cars, was to make its way by the lake road, and was to secure the power station, government offices and police station. The

plan was for the river-borne force to embark at the Ashar wharf at 4 a.m., with the land column arriving shortly thereafter. The whole operation was to be supported by aircraft on a pre-planned timetable between 4 and 5 a.m., and 6 and 7 a.m.

The hope that the early morning *coup de main* attack on the town would be a *fait accompli* proved to be wishful thinking. Ashar proved to be well defended, with a plethora of sniper posts scattered across the rooftops of the town, and Iraqi machine-guns and vehicles blocking the road between Ashar and Zubeila, the route by which the land column planned to enter the town. Whilst the river-borne assault met with good progress, the road column struck stiff resistance, although within hours all of the battalion's objectives had been captured, and some 34 armed policemen forced to surrender. However, it proved impossible to stamp out the heavy sniper fire that reverberated across the town, a situation that it was felt could only be resolved by a laborious house clearance operation, which would not be possible with the limited number of troops available. As the day drew on, it and the sniper attacks continued unabated it was decided to threaten the town with attack by artillery unless these attacks ceased. The threat worked, and cautious Gurkha patrols felt their way slowly into the town during the afternoon. By the end of the day armoured patrols of 2/7 Gurkha had managed to enter and to occupy the town without further incident. Gurkha casualties totalled four killed and nine wounded. Later in the afternoon 2/4 Gurkha were loaded onto HMS *Cockchafer* and HMS *Yennan* and landed at Ashar early on 8 May. During the day Ashar firmly came under British control, and with the exception of some incidents of looting, the situation was calm by the evening, and marked the end of operations to secure the Basra and Shaibah areas.

The effort to land and establish a division in the Basra area, and there to form a base from which future operations in Iraq could be launched and the Iranian oil refinery at Abadan protected, proved to be a considerable achievement. However, because no transport had yet arrived from India and the Iraqis had worked hard to deny the transport

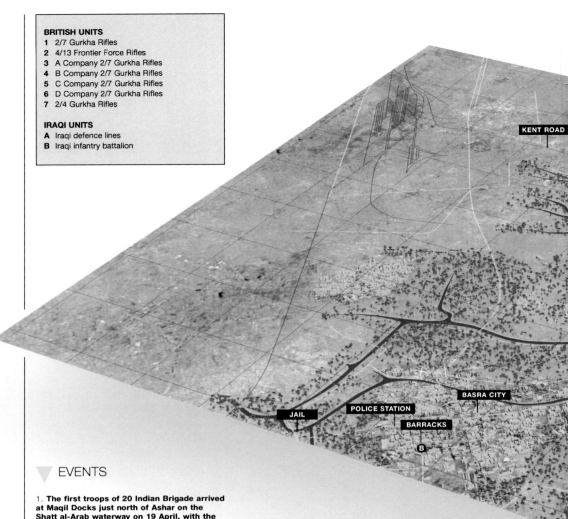

BRITISH UNITS
1 2/7 Gurkha Rifles
2 4/13 Frontier Force Rifles
3 A Company 2/7 Gurkha Rifles
4 B Company 2/7 Gurkha Rifles
5 C Company 2/7 Gurkha Rifles
6 D Company 2/7 Gurkha Rifles
7 2/4 Gurkha Rifles

IRAQI UNITS
A Iraqi defence lines
B Iraqi infantry battalion

ZUBEILA BARRAC

KENT ROAD

LAKE ROAD

ASHAR CREEK

BASRA CITY

JAIL

POLICE STATION

BARRACKS

B

▼ EVENTS

1. The first troops of 20 Indian Brigade arrived at Maqil Docks just north of Ashar on the Shatt al-Arab waterway on 19 April, with the remainder of the battalion arriving on 29 April, just at the start of hostilities with Iraq. The town of Ashar was a critical feature, as it dominated the Shatt al-Arab as well as providing access to Basra itself, and needed to be secured. But because of the weakness of 20 Brigade, the seizure of Ashar had to be postponed until the arrival of 21 Indian Brigade, which arrived on 6 May. An operation to capture Ashar was planned for the following day.

2. A platoon of 2/7 Gurkha Rifles was placed to guard the Rafidain Oil Company Depot on the west bank, north of Ashar, earlier in the week.

3. The attack on Ashar began before dawn on 7 May. A river-borne force comprising HQ, B and C companies of 2/7 Gurkha Rifles landed at the wharf and quickly secured the river bank.

4. At the same time a column of troops comprising A and D companies of 2/7 Gurkha Rifles, together with three Rolls Royce armoured cars of the 13th lancers, moved out of Maqil along the 'lake' road through Zubeila, to attack Ashar from the west. The 2/4 Gurkha Rifles were to remain in reserve near Zubeila during the day.

5. It became quickly apparent that Ashar was well defended. Iraqi troops with machine-guns guarded the Lake Road and inflicted a number of casualties on the advancing Gurkhas. It took most of the remaining part of the morning for the Gurkhas to push the Iraqis back into Ashar, from where the Iraqis maintained steady sniper-led attacks on the British.

6. Likewise, although the wharf had been quickly secured, the Iraqis had defended the Ashar Creek frontage very effectively, with machine-guns and snipers liberally positioned across rooftops and in the streets. It was apparent that Ashar would not be a push-over if the Iraqis decided to defend it aggressively, as they appeared willing to do.

7. By early afternoon the column advancing from Zubeila had captured the Power Station, Police Station and Telegraph Office, linking up with the remainder of the battalion which had arrived by river. The brigade commander then managed to communicate with the senior Iraqi commander in Ashar, and persuaded him of the futility of resisting, promising that if his men continued to fight the guns of 3 Field Regiment Royal Artillery (at Maqil) would be ranged on the town. This threat was sufficient to persuade the Iraqis in the town to surrender or melt away into the civilian population, and by the evening Ashar was in the hands of 2/7 Gurkha Rifles.

8. Early on 8 May the whole of 2/4 Gurkha Rifles were moved from Zubeila to the river front, embarked on river-craft, and brought into Ashar as reinforcements. A company of 4/13 Frontier Force Rifles accompanied them, a platoon of which relieved the platoon of 2/7 Gurkhas guarding the oil refinery. As a result of this successful attack on Ashar, Basra was secured without a fight, although Iraqi resistance, both by armed police and Iraqi Army units, continued until 17 May.

CAPTURE OF ASHAR 7 MAY 1941

For the British it was considered vital to secure the Basra–Shaibah area in case reinforcements were required for the comparatively small British forces in the region. Ashar was a key target in this strategy and the British advance on the town met considerable resistance.

Note: Gridlines are shown at intervals of 500 metres

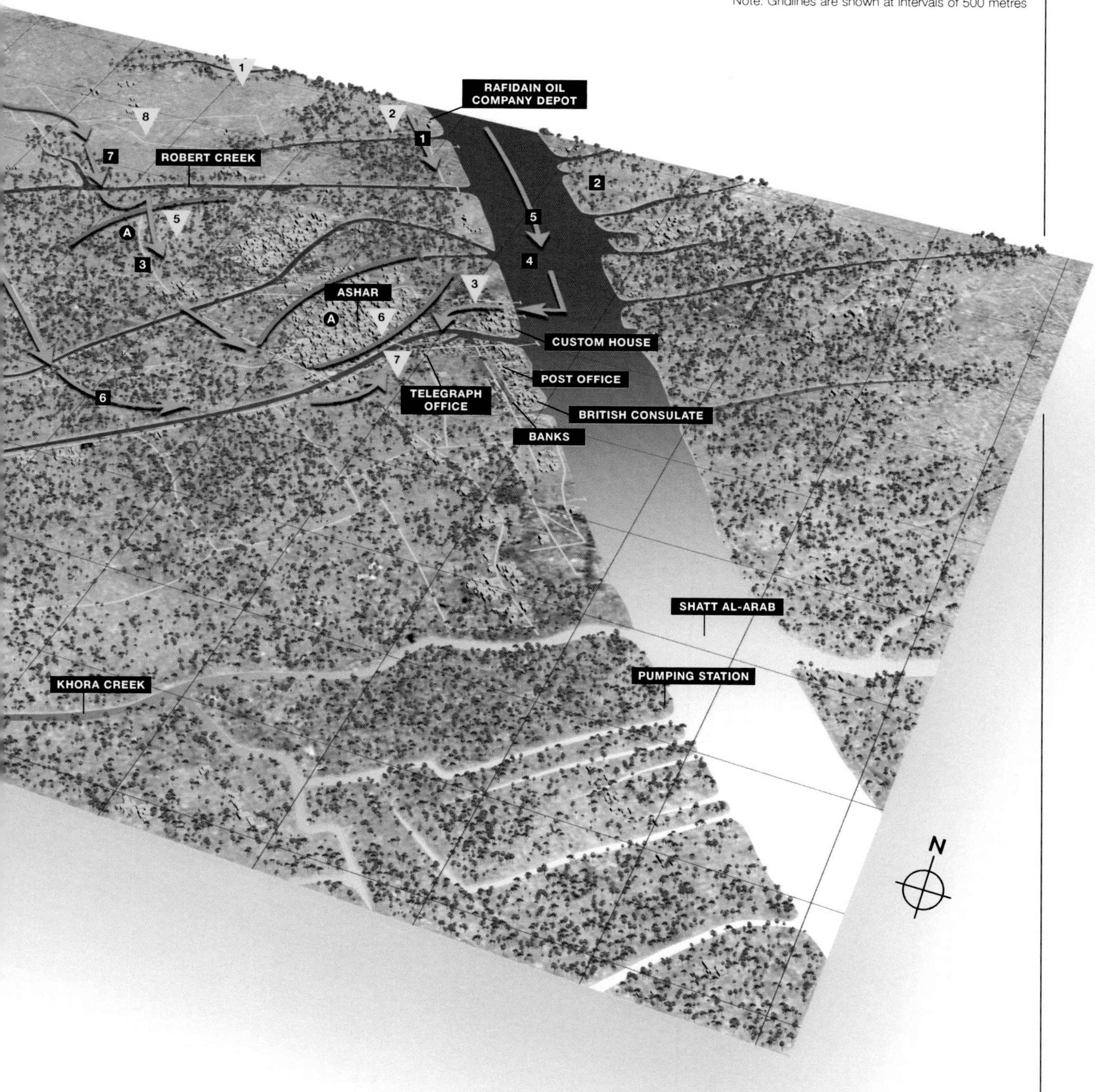

RAFIDAIN OIL
COMPANY DEPOT

ROBERT CREEK

ASHAR

CUSTOM HOUSE

POST OFFICE

TELEGRAPH
OFFICE

BRITISH CONSULATE

BANKS

SHATT AL-ARAB

PUMPING STATION

KHORA CREEK

N

routes north-west towards Baghdad, locomotives and river-craft being removed northwards and rail and telegraph lines uprooted and destroyed, it was clear that the relief of Habbaniya could not come from this source. Both 20 and 21 Indian Brigades and the HQ of 10 Indian Division gradually established a firm base in the Basra area and through offensive action across the region removed any threat of Iraqi interference in operations to the north. This was by no means what Auchinleck had wished but a useful role was played nevertheless by the two brigades, subduing localized dissent and sponsoring the creation of regional government favourable to the rule of the Regent. While 20 Indian Brigade was given responsibility for the defence of Shaibah, 21 Indian Brigade protected Basra itself and the port area. The division was complete when on 30 May the final of its three brigades – 25 Infantry Brigade (3 Jat Regiment, 2 Royal Sikh Regiment and 1 Mahratta Light Infantry) – disembarked from its convoy in Basra port.

THE BATTLE FOR HABBANIYA

The arrival of the second convoy in Basra on 29 April came as a severe shock to Rashid Ali. Cornwallis deliberately refrained from passing him the diplomatic note informing Iraq of the imminent arrival of the remainder of Fraser's troops until the day before. Rashid Ali was by now a very nervous man, pestering the Axis powers on 26 and 28 April for substantial military aid and financial support. The Iraqis asked for captured British infantry weapons with which the Iraqi Army were familiar, including 400 0.5in Boys armour-piercing rifles (with 50,000 rounds of ammunition), 60 armour-piercing cannons (with 60,000 rounds of ammunition), 10,000 hand grenades, 600 Bren guns and 84 Vickers heavy machine-guns.

Rashid Ali's instinctive reaction to Cornwallis' note was to refuse the British request outright, relying on the expectation of German intervention. Cornwallis, however, refused to budge, insisting that the troops would unload as planned under the terms of the treaty between the two countries, and that any intervention by Iraq to prevent this would be regarded by Great Britain as a hostile act. By now the atmosphere in Baghdad was tense and threatening and on 29 April Cornwallis ordered the evacuation of 250 British women and children from Baghdad to Habbaniya.

There was also a dramatic increase in anti-British rhetoric and hostility amongst the populace. Late in the afternoon of 29 April large

A scene from the Embassy in Baghdad during the siege. Because of the heat and the overcrowding in the Embassy itself, people slept in the grounds. The traveller and diarist, Freya Stark, wrote an engaging account of her time as a prisoner in the Embassy, in *East is West* (John Murray, 1945). (IWM E3448)

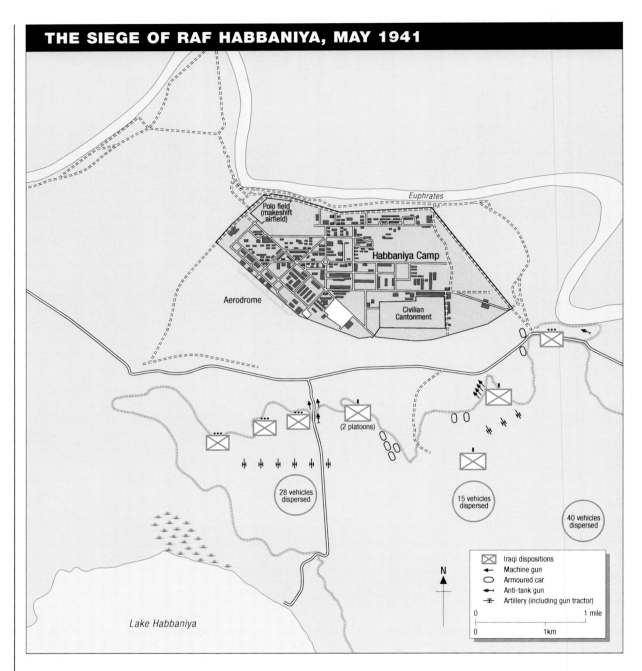

Euphrates

Polo field (makeshift airfield)

Habbaniya Camp

Aerodrome

Civilian Cantonment

(2 platoons)

28 vehicles dispersed

15 vehicles dispersed

40 vehicles dispersed

N

	Iraqi dispositions
	Machine gun
	Armoured car
	Anti-tank gun
	Artillery (including gun tractor)

0   1 mile

0   1km

Lake Habbaniya

numbers of Iraqi soldiers streamed out of Baghdad westward along the road towards the Euphrates at Falluja and beyond. Simultaneously the Euphrates embankments were cut, which acted to flood the low lying areas around Habbaniya and effectively cut it off from the east. The British Embassy reported these troop movements at 3 a.m. on the morning of 30 April. During that day an estimated two brigades of Iraqi troops made their way towards Habbaniya and a further brigade occupied the town of Ramadi, 14 miles west of Habbaniya on the Euphrates. The troops involved had been instructed to deploy on a training exercise to the high ground between Lake Habbaniya and the

A Wellington Mk 1c of No. 37 Sqn over the desert. These aircraft played a decisive role in the destruction of the RIAF in May 1941. (IWM CM501)

Cantonment. The only thing to arouse the suspicions of the inquisitive was the fact that they were also told to take live ammunition. In Baghdad tension mounted and some 350 British subjects fled for safety to the British Embassy, whilst the American Legation provided shelter for another 150. The Iraqis then placed the British Embassy under a virtual state of siege and the road from Baghdad to Falluja was closed. Iraqi troops simultaneously seized the oilfields at Kirkuk, promptly shutting down the flow of oil to Haifa and opening up that to Tripoli, a flow that Britain had originally closed down with the collapse of France nearly a year before. Rashid Ali's intention was to place RAF Habbaniya under a state of siege, in the hope that this would force Britain out of Iraq without a fight, the fear of a bloodbath at the cantonment being sufficient, he believed, to frighten the British into withdrawal.

The news, therefore, in the early hours of 30 April of the troop deployments from Baghdad caused the general alarm to be sounded at 4.20 a.m. As the early dawn broke just over half an hour later it was with considerable consternation that the Habbaniya garrison discovered that it was being overlooked from the escarpment by a large number of troops, clearly visible to the naked eye, preparing defensive positions. An Audax sent up to report came back with the information that at least 1,000 troops with field guns, howitzers and armoured vehicles were dispersed across the plateau and long lines of vehicles could be seen on the road that stretched back towards Falluja and, beyond that, Baghdad. That first day it was estimated that the Iraqis had deployed on the escarpment:

Three infantry battalions
An artillery brigade
12 Crossley six-wheeled armoured cars
A mechanized machine-gun company
A number of Fiat light tanks

In addition, at Falluja were thought to be an infantry company and on the road between Falluja and Baghdad one horsed infantry brigade. **39**

By 2 May the Iraqi force on the escarpment had expanded to 9,000 troops with 28 guns and armoured cars.

AVM Smart had no time to consider his options before an Iraqi officer arrived at the main gate at 6 a.m. with the following message:

> For the purposes of training we have occupied the Habbaniya hills. Please make no flying or the going out of any force or persons from the cantonment. If any aircraft or armoured car attempts to go out it will be shelled by our batteries, and we will not be responsible for it.

Undoubtedly struck by the incongruity of a training exercise conducted with live ammunition, Smart had the presence of mind to reply:

> Any interference with training flights will be considered an 'act of war' and will be met by immediate counter-offensive action. We demand the withdrawal of the Iraqi forces from positions which are clearly hostile and must place my camp at their mercy.

The Iraqi action placed Smart in a quandary. Despite the rapid decline in formal relations between Great Britain and Iraq over the previous month, Smart was not expecting any form of military threat to develop against Habbaniya. The 364 soldiers of the King's Own had arrived by air from Shaibah on 29 April but, even with the six companies of the Iraq Levies, the total ground forces available to him amounted to a mere 1,550, strengthened by 18 thin-skinned Rolls Royce armoured cars of No. 1 Company RAF. These vehicles were amongst the last of a consignment of ex-Royal Navy cars that had been serving in the Middle East since 1915. Nevertheless it was plain to Smart that an aggressive defence of Habbaniya was required, and that to do nothing would leave the initiative with the Iraqis.

During that day, one of intense but dry heat with the mercury well over 110 degrees Fahrenheit, frantic preparations for battle took place across the cantonment. Two Imperial Airways flying boats managed to take off from Lake Habbaniya in the morning, leaving six airline employees behind. They were taken prisoner by the Iraqis in the afternoon. Trenches were dug to ensure that if shelling did begin some shelter could be had in the otherwise entirely defenceless station. Whilst troops and aircrew were pressed into this task, the pilots manoeuvred the aircraft out of sight of the Iraqi guns and a battle roster was organized. The aircraft of the 'Air Striking Force' were split into two groups. The 21 Audax 'bombers' were placed under command of Wing Commander C.W.M 'Larry' Ling and were to operate from the polo field out of sight of the Iraqis on the plateau whilst the remaining 43 aircraft under Squadron Leader Tony Dudgeon were to operate from the main runway in full view of the enemy. Dudgeon's group comprised a flight of 27 Oxfords, a second flight of nine Gladiators (flying from the polo field) and a third flight of seven Gordons. The lack of suitably trained pilots, however, was acute. Eventually, only 39 were found, some of whom had not flown for a considerable period of time and many of whom had never flown in battle before, 18 to fly the Audaxes and 19 for the remainder. Some, members of the Royal Hellenic Air Force on a flying training course, could not even speak English. Within 14 hours of the start of battle a quarter of these pilots had been lost.

The likely opposition in the air was formidable. The RIAF had a substantial and modern air force with many British-trained pilots. They boasted seven squadrons with over 70 operational aircraft, including Italian Savoia 79 tri-engine bombers and Italian Breda 65 fighters, American Northrop fighters and Audaxes with more powerful engines than the British version (named the Hawker Nisr).

During the first day of the siege, Smart waited for clear instructions from Cornwallis at the Embassy in Baghdad, and from Cairo. In the morning he told Cornwallis by telegraph that Iraqi artillery pieces were being aimed directly at the base and that enemy troop numbers were increasing. Then, at 11.30 a.m. the Iraqi military envoy returned to the front gate. He now stated that training flights had to cease, citing Britain's blatant disregard for the Anglo-Iraq Treaty for this new demand, undoubtedly referring to the second Basra landing on 29 April. This put Smart in a very difficult position. He knew that he was extremely vulnerable to ground attack, and that if he were to retain the initiative he would have to launch his own pre-emptive attack before the Iraqis felt that they were in a position of complete dominance. On the other side of the coin, a pre-emptive air strike could not guarantee that the Iraqi forces would not retaliate against the vulnerable cantonment. At least 250 women and children, shipped hastily out of Baghdad in RAF trucks the day before, were still on the base, as well as the large civilian population, many of whom were Iraqis, whose reactions to firm military action by Smart were difficult to gauge. The only certainty was that Habbaniya was vulnerable and likely to become more so if he did nothing about it.

In the absence of instructions, Smart decided to play for time. He was fearful, in the absence of clear orders, of starting his own private war. At midday he gave the Iraqi envoy his answer, which was a polite request to remove his forces from the plateau and to let their respective political

Air defences at RAF Habbaniya consisted of Lewis guns in sand-bagged emplacements. (Mel Meluish via RAF Habbaniya Association)

masters on either side sort out the impasse. By this time 27 guns could be counted on the escarpment, only one shell from which could disable the water tower or destroy the power station, which would bring the defence of Habbaniya to a sudden and ignominious end. Habbaniya could not, in any case, have withstood a lengthy siege, as it had rations for the civilian cantonment for a mere four days, and only 12 days for the garrison. Immediately following this meeting, Smart sent his third signal of the day to Cornwallis, repeating his request for reinforcements and asking for a firm directive.

During the next day – 1 May 1941 – the need for Smart to launch a pre-emptive strike against the Iraqi forces on the escarpment became clearer. The Foreign Office in London instructed Cornwallis to take what steps he thought were necessary to seize the initiative. Auchinleck signalled to the effect that he believed that Smart should attack at once, although MajGen Fraser in Basra told him that he would be unable to assist as the Iraqis had breached the flood defences and had made northward movement by his troops on land impossible. Immediate aid for Habbaniya would not be forthcoming from the lone Indian brigade now in Basra. Smart wanted to ensure that, if he did launch military action, he had the whole day available to prepare. He therefore asked Cornwallis to declare an ultimatum to the Iraqis, giving them three hours to withdraw, and delivering the message at 5 a.m. local time on the morning of 2 May. Cornwallis replied at midday to the effect that the time for ultimatums was past, and that he had advised London that he was expecting air action against the Iraqis on the escarpment at Habbaniya that very day. Finally realizing the danger of the situation in Iraq, Longmore in Cairo on 1 May ordered 18 Wellingtons from Egypt to Shaibah (eight from No. 70 Squadron and ten from No. 37 Squadron) to supplement the single Wellington and six Gladiators that had arrived from the Middle East on 19 April. A telegram from Churchill with advice that was characteristic and uncompromising, strengthened his resolve: '*If you have to strike, strike hard. Use all necessary force.*'

At a conference held at 8 p.m. that night, Smart briefed his officers. They would attack at 5 a.m. the next morning, with eight of the newly arrived Wellington bombers from Basra joining in. The aim was to secure complete surprise with the heaviest bombing that could be brought to bear on the Iraqi positions across the escarpment. At 2.45 a.m. Smart sent the local Iraqi commander an ultimatum to the effect that if his forces were not withdrawn forthwith he would be forced to take immediate action. No response to this ultimatum was received.

In the relative coolness of the pre-dawn darkness on 2 May 1941 the aircraft, parked on the main runway and the polo field facing their direction of take-off, were prepared for action. Lifting into the still inky darkness just before 5 a.m., the entire armed aircraft complement at Habbaniya launched itself one by one into the air. Once airborne, the aircraft grouped above the plateau, joining the Wellingtons that had travelled 300 miles north-west from Basra, and then threw themselves determinedly against the Iraqi positions. The objectives of the attack were artillery, machine-gun positions and armoured vehicles, although, as the day progressed, any suitable target was attacked. The principal aim was to hit the Iraqis hard enough to prevent a ground assault on the otherwise defenceless base. Sqn Ldr Tony Dudgeon recalled the confusion of the skies above the escarpment during those first few hours:

> As the daylight got stronger we could see that the air above the plateau was like the front of a wasp's nest on a sunny morning. The ten Wellingtons were there from Basrah [sic] making a total of forty-nine aircraft of five different types and speeds, clustering and jockeying over an area not much bigger than a minor golf course. It was a hairy experience. In my Oxford I would peer down into the dusk, trying to distinguish a juicy target like a gun-emplacement – and an Audax would swoop past at some crazy angle. Or a Wellington would sail majestically across my bows, giving me heart failure and leaving my machine bucketing about in its slipstream. Luckily, no one hit anybody else, but there were some very close shaves indeed.

To those waiting anxiously inside the cantonment, the planes seemed to skim over the plateau, Iraqi small-arms and anti-aircraft fire reaching out to touch them, while clouds of dust and smoke billowed skywards from the bomb strikes.

The attack came entirely as a surprise to the Iraqi forces on the escarpment, as it was intended. Despite the live ammunition they carried, many soldiers still thought that they were on a training exercise. For their part, the fact that the British were prepared to fight rather than negotiate a peaceful surrender came to Rashid Ali and the Golden Square as something of a shock. It was simply not what they had expected. To compound it all, the first attacks took place on Friday, and the largely Muslim army were preparing for morning prayers. On news of the attacks reaching Baghdad, an enraged Grand Mufti immediately declared a *jihad* against Great Britain and the flow of oil through the remaining pipeline to Haifa was severed through the sequestration of the Iraq Petroleum Company oil plants.

One of the blockhouses protecting RAF Habbaniya. (Fletcher via RAF Habbaniya Association)

Nevertheless, Iraqi artillery was quick to retaliate, shells firing indiscriminately into the cantonment only minutes after the first bombs began to fall. In the early half-light of the morning these guns revealed their positions by their muzzle flashes and proved easy targets for the bombers overhead. A routine now began. As aircraft divested themselves of their bombs they would scoot back to Habbaniya, either to the airfield or to the polo ground, and, whilst one of the crew would bomb-up, the other would rush to the operations room to report on the last sortie and receive target instructions for the next. Any halt to the operation would invite attack from the ground, and everyone fighting that day at Habbaniya knew that they had to keep the bombardment going without end until the Iraqis broke.

Pupils and ground crew volunteered to act as crew for the departing aircraft and the novice bomb-aimers and machine-gunners proved remarkably accurate. During that first day of battle, several aircraft were lost,

including a Wellington, which managed to land on the airfield but was hit by Iraqi artillery and destroyed. Many others were peppered with holes from bullet strikes. Additionally, Iraqi Northrops, Bredas, Savoias, Audaxes and Gladiators made a number of attacks on Habbaniya, bombing and strafing relatively inaccurately. The only anti-aircraft defences Habbaniya could boast were Lewis guns on mounts and protected by sandbags, no match for high-speed, multi-gun Iraqi monoplane fighters. On the ground strong offensive action had also taken place by the Levies and troops of the King's Own to identify enemy gun emplacements and to cover the perimeter with machine-guns from the blockhouses that were sited around the base.

These efforts involved fighting patrols sent out to locate and destroy an enemy gun emplacement behind the Burma Bund across the Euphrates by No. 8 (Kurdish) Company of the Levies and action by No. 4 (Assyrian) Company successfully to repel a foray towards the camp from the south early in the day by eight Iraqi armoured cars and three light tanks using anti-tank rifles. The patrol from the Kurdish Company managed to cross the Euphrates by means of an old motorboat, although it soon came under heavy machine-gun fire from Iraqi positions on the northern bank, which prevented it from getting to its objective. However, aircraft from Habbaniya managed successfully to bomb the positions later in the day and the guns were silenced. The blockhouses around the perimeter had good fields of fire. One of them (No. 10) had excellent views across to the Falluja road, which it used to good effect, shooting up traffic on the road during the day. Despite their conspicuousness, none was put out of action during the siege, although No. 8 remained under virtually continuous machine-gun fire and No. 9 had its front knocked in by an Iraqi shell. It continued to function unheeded. Aggressive action during this first day did much to temper Iraqi ardour and no further penetrations by armour were attempted against the perimeter during the siege. The blockhouses kept up a

Mk 1 Blenheims flying over the Euphrates. The arrival of four of these fast, modern aircraft from Palestine on Sunday 4 May made a welcome enhancement to the 'stringbags' that had hitherto made up the Habbaniya 'Air Striking Force'. (IWM CH135)

constant fire on all observed Iraqi movement and, although Iraqi artillery targeted these positions, they were surprisingly ineffective. None was put out of action.

As dusk fell late on that first day of fighting and the darkness stopped operational sorties until the morning, Smart evaluated the results. They were worrying. The Iraqis were still on the plateau, apparently unmoved. The only consolation to the scattered and vastly outnumbered infantrymen guarding Habbaniya was that there was no sign yet of a ground assault developing. Of the 64 aircraft that had begun the day, 22 had been shot down and ten of the 39 pilots had been killed or wounded. Two Vincent bombers had also been shot down during a sortie near Shaibah. During 14 hours of flying, 193 official sorties were counted – about six for each aircraft – but according to Dudgeon many more went unrecorded.

During the first night, the aircraft helpless on the ground, the Iraqi gunners lobbed some 200 shells into the cantonment between midnight and 3 a.m., fortunately without hitting the precious water tower or electricity generator and causing only a small number of casualties. The airbase facilities had no back-up, and, if the water tower or electric plant had been hit, life would have very quickly become extremely uncomfortable for the besieged. During the siege damage was done to the Assyrian and all three British churches, as well as some messes and billets, but miraculously nothing of practical importance was hit. Significantly, the large numbers of civilians showed little signs of panic during the siege. Despite this bombardment, aircraft were repaired and bombed up in preparation for another assault at dawn on the morning of Saturday 3 May. Morale was raised that night by the sound of Iraqi aeroplanes bombing their own positions at Ramadi, further to the west, by mistake. During the night Habbaniya's hard-pressed infantrymen and RAF armoured cars sent out fighting patrols to dominate 'no man's land' around the perimeter and successfully frightened off Iraqi patrols. Thereafter the Iraqis kept their distance at night, withdrawing their standing patrols at dusk and making little or no attempt in the days or nights that followed to raid the cantonment.

One of the First World War vintage artillery field pieces on display in front of Air Headquarters at RAF Habbaniya, before the war. These weapons were cleaned up, provided with new firing mechanisms, and pressed into action during May 1941. (J Walker via RAF Habbaniya Association)

SqnLdr Tony Dudgeon's Airspeed Oxford Mark 1 undergoing pre-flight checks before a raid on 5 May 1941. It has been adjusted to carry 8 x 20lb AP bombs. The navigator, Sgt Arthur Prickett, is underneath the aircraft checking the bombs. He was killed the following day, the last day of the siege. (IWM HU63836)

On the second day of the battle the re-organized squadrons at Habbaniya were made ready at 4 a.m. for a 5 a.m. lift-off. On this day the DC2s of 31 Squadron, temporarily based at Basra, flew in to take off the remaining women and children and fly them to Basra and then India. As the slow and defenceless transport aircraft flew into Habbaniya, Audaxes flew violent sorties against the Iraqi positions to prevent them targeting the lumbering planes and their precious cargoes. RAF armoured cars would race down the airfield alongside the aircraft as they gathered speed, offering what close-range protection they could from Iraqi ground attack.

Fortunately, on 1 May, the highly competent Col Ouvry Roberts, who was to command a division at the battle of Imphal under General Slim later in the war, flew into Habbaniya from Basra in a Vincent with instructions to establish contact between the two bases and to report the situation back to Fraser. It was not his intention to remain in Habbaniya but, pressed nevertheless by WgCdre Hawtrey and others to stay, he did so and took effective command on Smart's departure.

During Saturday 3 May aerial attacks from Habbaniya were extended to include not just the immediate presence of Iraqi forces on the escarpment,

Wrecked Iraqi artillery on the escarpment overlooking Habbaniya. (IWM CM812)

A wrecked Iraqi position, with a panoramic view overlooking Habbaniya. The problem was that these trenches were not ideal locations for infantry weapons and machine-gun pits were good targets for the roving aircraft of the RAF's 'Air Striking Force'. (IWM CM809)

Iraqi dead at Habbaniya being gathered for burial by POWs in the days immediately following the end of the battle of the escarpment on 7 May. (IWM CM807)

but Iraqi airfields around Baghdad and the Baghdad–Falluja–Ramadi road along which the forces on the escarpment were receiving supplies and reinforcements. Three Wellingtons of No. 37 Squadron off-loaded some 7,100 pounds of explosives onto Rashid airfield in Baghdad. On Sunday 4 May eight Wellingtons continued the attack, dropping 15,700 pounds, destroying hangars, dispersed aircraft, magazines and ground defences. Entirely unexpectedly, four Blenheim twin-engined fighters from 203 Squadron arrived from Egypt, making a powerful and welcome addition to the offensive capability of the base. These aircraft conducted an immediate low-level machine-gun attack on Rashid airfield and Baghdad civil airport. These attacks proved extremely effective in limiting the offensive capability of the Iraqi Air Force and in severely undermining the fragile morale of Iraqi troops on the ground. In the days that followed, attacks continued against Iraqi airfields in Baghdad and at Ba'quba (north of the city) with considerable success, and against Iraqi vehicles attempting to supply the troops on the plateau. All the while the Iraqi guns on the plateau fired indiscriminately but relatively ineffectively into the Habbaniya compound.

Iraqi artillery destroyed at Sin-el-Dhibban village following fierce fighting on 6 May. (IWM E3324)

That night attempts were made to prevent Iraqi artillery firing on the cantonment during the hours of darkness. A blackout was imposed across the cantonment, and delayed-action bombs were also dropped by aircraft during the day, designed to explode at various times during the night. Additionally, although possessing neither night navigational instruments nor lights, a number of aircrew flew sorties against the plateau at night, a hazardous undertaking that cost the lives of at least one Oxford crew. Aircraft had to take-off blind, the pilot trusting to experience to judge when to lift off, and landing solely with the support of the landing light switched on briefly shortly before landing.

At dawn the following morning – Sunday 4 May – attacks continued unabated from both Habbaniya and Shaibah. An attack on Rashid Airfield was devastating for the Iraqi Air Force, costing it some 29 aircraft. A further 13 were lost at Ba'quba. Leaflets were also dropped over Baghdad, assuring the population that Britain's argument was only with the usurper government, and the Regent broadcast from Jerusalem appealing to the population not to be led astray by 'falsehood and lies which had brought the country from the blessings of peace to the horrors of a venomous war.'

Two elderly First World War-vintage 18-pdr field guns graced the entrance to Air Headquarters (AHQ) at Habbaniya. They had not been used in anger since fighting the Turks and it was assumed that they had been disabled. Fortunately, this was not so. Although they had been decommissioned for over two decades and had been painted liberally over the years, Roberts believed that it could be possible to press them back into service. They were stripped and cleaned by a Royal Artillery artificer flown in from Basra, and 4.5in ammunition arrived courtesy of the 31 Squadron DC2s. Not only did the weapons work but they proved to be surprisingly effective. The BBC ran a special report for propaganda purposes explaining that specially equipped aircraft had flown in heavy artillery.

Iraqi equipment destroyed on road to Falluja on 6 May 1941 following ferocious air attacks by the RAF Habbaniya 'Air Striking Force'. (IWM E3322)

During the siege, 31 Squadron worked wonders to fly in under the noses of the enemy guns every day to bring in supplies and reinforcements, and to evacuate wounded and non-combatants to Shaibah. On 6 May, however, two Valentias, carrying two platoons of the King's Own, became lost over the desert and landed next to a pumping station that was in the hands of the Iraqi Army. The pilot of the first Valentia, on realizing his mistake, managed to take off, but the second aircraft became stuck in the sand. Frantic efforts to dig the aircraft out failed, and after machine-gun fire from the Iraqi fort had set the plane on fire, the British troops were forced to surrender.

Four full days of fighting provided a heavy toll on Habbaniya's dwindling air force. By the evening of Monday 5 May only four of the Oxfords were 'flyable' and virtually all of the remaining aircraft had been patched up liberally with fabric patches pasted over bullet holes.

Until this time there had been no indication that the British attacks had made any significant impact on the Iraqi troops manning the positions on the escarpment, although the Iraqis continued to make

Civilians in the US Legation armed with shotguns and pistols. Mr Paul Knabenshue, the US consul, allowed some 150 British expatriates to take refuge in the 'White House on the Tigris', as the legation was colloquially called. Mr Knabenshue was instrumental in allowing the Regent to escape his would be murderers on 1 April 1941. (IWM E3454)

little use of their tremendous topographical advantage. The infantrymen and armoured cars defending the base were stretched, concentrating on manning the blockhouses with their antiquated Lewis guns and dominating the ground around Habbaniya at night. On 5 May a patrol of the King's Own failed to drive off the Iraqi troops defending Sin el-Dhibban village (Arabic for 'Teeth of the Wolf'), four miles south of the cantonment and the vital ferry point over the Euphrates, which the Iraqis were using to reinforce their positions on the escarpment. Some 200 Iraqis were reported to be strongly entrenched in well-defended positions around the village.

On the morning of Tuesday 6 May, it became clear from aerial reconnaissance that a massive reinforcement of the plateau was underway. This news was accompanied by the heaviest raid by the Iraqi Air Force to date, and it appeared that an all-out effort was about to be made to finish off the Habbaniya defenders. Then, unaccountably, the forces on the plateau decided that they had had enough, and began to stream away from their positions. Signals intelligence indicated that Rashid Ali was appealing urgently for Axis support. The unremitting British air attacks, coupled with the fact that the Iraqi troops had deployed without rations or fresh water, had led to a dramatic loss of morale on the escarpment. It may also have been the case that some of the soldiers, as a number indicated afterwards to Glubb Pasha, had never been entirely comfortable with waging war on their erstwhile allies.

The withdrawal of troops from the escarpment was not followed by the troops at Sin-el-Dhibban, who proved more difficult to budge. During the day three successive attacks by B and D Companies of the King's Own and the Levies, supported by the Rolls Royce armoured cars, finally forced the remaining defenders from the village. D Company lost four men killed and four wounded, whilst B Company lost one man killed. Then, at about 4 p.m., troop reinforcements with armoured vehicles were spotted heading for the ferry point from the area of Falluja. Every available aircraft was thrown into the sky to meet this new threat. 'We made 139 aircraft sorties' Dudgeon recalled, 'and, when the last aircraft left, its pilot reported that the road was a strip of flames, several hundred

This magnificent painting by the late Frank Wootten commemorates the pre-emptive strikes made by No.4 Service Training School on the Iraqi brigade positions overlooking RAF Habbaniya between 1 and 7 May 1941. The scene shows the situation at 9 a.m. on the first morning of the battle. The Iraqi positions were first attacked by aircraft from both RAF Habbaniya and RAF Shaibah (near Basra) at dawn. Wellington bombers jostled with silver Hawker Audaxes and Oxford trainers to bomb and machine-gun the Iraqi positions in the high ground below them. The Oxford marked 'D' is flown by Squadron Leader Tony Dudgeon. The three crewmen in the Oxford seen falling in flames were killed. The smoke from a Wellington bomber which exploded on the runway at Habbaniya after being hit by artillery fire whilst taxiing can be seen clearly. Black puffs of Iraqi anti-aircraft fire can also be seen, but machine-gun and rifle fire caused most casualties, puncturing most of the aircraft that flew. In the first 14 hours of the battle a quarter of the aircrew engaged and a third of the aircraft had been lost. (Officers' Mess, No.4 Flying Training School, RAF Valley)

yards long. There were ammunition limbers exploding, with cars and lorries burning by the dozen. We lost one Audax shot down.' The Iraqis retaliated with an air attack at 5 p.m., destroying two Oxfords, a Gladiator and an Audax, and killing seven and wounding eight.

The end of the siege was close. During 6 May troops of the garrison took 408 prisoners. The estimate of Iraqi losses was put at anything between 500 and 1,000, although precise figures are impossible now to estimate. The plunder seized from the escarpment was substantial and provided a welcome relief for Roberts. The garrison captured six Czech-built 3.7in howitzers with 2,400 shells, an 18-pdr gun, one Italian tank, 10 British Crossley armoured cars, 79 trucks, three 20mm anti-aircraft guns with 2,500 shells, 45 Bren light machine-guns, 11 Vickers heavy machine-guns, 340 rifles and 500,000 rounds of ammunition. The light arms were all British and far superior to those with which either the Indian Army or British troops in Palestine were equipped, having to rely on ancient Lewis and Hotchkiss guns their fathers and grandfathers had used in an earlier era.

On Wednesday 7 May RAF armoured cars reconnoitred the top of the plateau and reported it deserted. The siege was over. It had been an extraordinary week. 'During those hectic 5 days', Dudgeon calculated, 'our hastily armed, outdated training machines had dropped well over 3,000 bombs, totalling over 50 tons, and we had fired 116,000 rounds of ammunition. The ops-room had recorded 647 sorties, but we had completed, unrecorded, many more than that... Our losses [from 4 Training School] were 13 killed and 21 too badly wounded to carry on – and 4 more grounded from nerves gone.' Losses from pilots and crews from other units who joined the battle on an *ad hoc* basis were never recorded. Habbaniya's gallant defenders had achieved an extraordinary victory. Through their bold and determined attacks they had gained moral ascendancy over both the Rashid Ali regime and the Iraqi armed forces. Churchill cabled the defenders of Habbaniya on 7 May 1941:

> *Your vigorous and splendid action has largely restored the situation. We are watching the grand fight you are making. All possible aid will be sent. Keep it up!*

Churchill's message was the first occasion that the defenders at Habbaniya had heard that a relief expedition was planned. If they believed that assistance was imminent, they were nevertheless to be disappointed, as a further week would elapse before the relief force was able to leave Palestine and a full 11 days before it arrived at Habbaniya.

In the two days following the debacle on the plateau, attacks from the air had virtually eradicated the remaining elements of the Iraqi Air Force, 13 aircraft being destroyed on the ground, and a further 20 damaged. Further reinforcements dribbled into Habbaniya over the ensuing days. On about 11 May five more superannuated Gladiator fighters from 94 Squadron arrived from Ismailia on the Suez Canal.

During the siege the besieged had heard nothing from the Embassy in Baghdad, and an attempt was made on the evening of 8 May to regain communication: an Audax dropped a message-bag into the Embassy garden. However, machine-gun fire prevented the same Audax from collecting a response using the tried-and-tested hook and cable method the following night, and so the base and the Embassy remained incommunicado.

The results of the Habbaniya battle were threefold. First, the cantonment was not over-run, and the defenders not defeated. Second, and as a consequence, Rashid Ali's assumed aim to use the threat to the cantonment as a bargaining chip in negotiations with Great Britain was decisively thwarted. That this political stratagem was Rashid Ali's aim was the most likely reason for the Iraqi failure to attack Habbaniya on 30 April and 1 May. It seems that Rashid Ali wanted to create a political crisis and to drag out the resulting impasse through negotiation. He did not believe for one moment that in its straitened circumstances Great Britain would defend its interests in Iraq by force, and thought that the resulting period of negotiation would give Germany time to bring arms and aircraft into the country. Third, in five days of incessant aerial bombardment the Iraqi army was dealt a devastating blow from which its morale never recovered. In the process, Iraq's air force was largely destroyed. The public standing of Rashid Ali's government was consequently dealt a severe blow, caused in part by its inability to overcome the Habbaniya problem or to ensure the timely arrival of the much-vaunted German legions, about which Rashid Ali had boasted for so long.

THE ADVANCE OF HABFORCE

Following Churchill's instructions on 3 May Wavell had immediately tasked MajGen George Clark, GOC 1 Cavalry Division and temporarily in command of Palestine, to assemble a column. It was to be called 'Habforce' – after its objective, RAF Habbaniya – and formed from whatever troops Clark had remaining following the earlier departure of 6 Infantry Division to both Greece and the Western Desert. Later that day Wavell reported the results of Clark's plans to London, concluding:

> *Very doubtful whether above force strong enough to relieve Habbaniya or whether Habbaniya can prolong resistance till its arrival. I am afraid I can only regard it as outside chance...*

Habforce comprised some 6,000 troops cobbled together from the remnants of troops available in Palestine and the Western Desert. The main force was based around Brig Joe Kingstone's 4 Cavalry Brigade. It was ill trained and poorly equipped. The Household Cavalry had only recently converted from horses to trucks and had seen no action to date. This transformation from horse to inferior trucked infantry with paltry training, and given the label 'mechanized', was itself a demoralizing experience for which the cavalrymen were unsurprisingly not very enthusiastic, especially when it involved shooting many of their horses. The problem was compounded by the fact that many of the troops were not in Palestine at all: the Royal Wiltshire Yeomanry was at Sidi Barrani

A mounted patrol from the Household Cavalry Regiment in Palestine, on 22 September 1940. The occasion was the last all-horsed exercise in British military history. (IWM E595)

His Majesty's Armoured Car 'Euphrates', a 1915-vintage Rolls Royce, part of No. 1 Armoured Car at RAF Habbaniya. (John Rolph via RAF Habbaniya)

in the Western Desert and 237 Battery had only recently arrived in Suez. After recall from the Western Desert, the three squadrons of the Royal Wiltshire Yeomanry covered 1,200 miles from Sidi Barrani to Habbaniya in nine days. Their role was to guard the line of communication between Palestine through Transjordan to Iraq against attacks by irregulars. As for the gunners of 237 Battery, although equipped with the fabulous 25-pdr gun, they had had no time to calibrate their weapons before going into action. The 1 Cavalry Division's operational role was internal security in Palestine, and thus found itself poorly prepared for a 500-mile adventure across the desert to Habbaniya.

In addition, Habforce included No. 2 Armoured Car Company RAF with eight Fordson armoured cars (modelled on the 1915 Rolls Royce Silver Spirit cars, with which the armoured car squadron at Habbaniya were equipped), commanded by Sqn Ldr Cassano, an anti-tank troop of the Royal Artillery with 2pdr guns, a troop of the 2 Field Squadron Royal Engineers and a detachment of 166 Field Ambulance. It had no tanks. On 5 May Cassano's armoured cars were 1,000 miles to the west, guarding airfields in the Western Desert. Habforce did not possess modern machine-guns. Parts of the British Army and most of the Indian Army were forced to soldier on with the ancient Hotchkiss, a weapon hated by the troops. The Household Cavalry Regiment was issued with 2-inch mortars – one per troop – for the first time on 9 May, but of course had no time to practise on them before they were used in anger against the enemy for the first time later in the month. Other equipment issued to the cavalrymen included bayonets for their rifles and one wireless set per squadron. Some of the trucks with which they had been issued in February and March had solid rubber tyres and appeared to have been stored in Egypt since the end of the First World War. With the rapid mechanization of the regiment, most of the drivers were newly trained. What they lacked in training and equipment, however, 'Habforce' made up for in an infectious though naïve enthusiasm for the adventure ahead.

The force was supported by Maj John Bagot Glubb, otherwise known as 'Glubb Pasha', as political officer, together with 350 men of the Desert Mechanized Regiment of the Arab Legion as his personal escort.

Troops of the Arab Legion's 'Desert Mechanized Regiment' at Rutbah Wells Fort inside Iraq on 14 May 1941. These men were ostensibly Glubb Pasha's personal escort during the campaign, but ended up doing their fair share of fighting. The day after this photograph was taken the Arab Legion departed with 'Kingcol' across the Iraqi desert for RAF Habbaniya. (IWM E2936E)

These armoured cars of the Arab Legion were made for the Legion by a German firm in Jaffa, Palestine. (IWM E345)

Equipped with 1915-vintage Lewis guns and equally decrepit Hotchkiss guns, they travelled in a mixture of civilian Ford trucks and home-made armoured cars. The Arab Legion was not part of the British Army, but was loaned to Wavell for the operation. The Emir of Transjordan, the brother of the Regent of Iraq, had a personal score to settle with Rashid Ali and his rebels. Habforce was also to be joined by a mechanized squadron of the Transjordan Frontier Force (TJFF), which, unlike the Arab Legion, was a British imperial unit, paid for by Great Britain and led by officers on loan from the British Army.

On 6 May Gen Sir Henry 'Jumbo' Wilson arrived in Jerusalem, following his evacuation from the debacle in Greece, to take command of British forces in Palestine. Clark briefed him on the plans made over the previous three days. AVM John D'Albiac, who had also been in Greece with Wilson, as Air Officer Commanding (AOC), had already arrived in Palestine. Wavell, Wilson, Clark and D'Albiac met in Jerusalem on

11 May to finalize plans for the operation, and it was here that Clark was told that his secondary objective was the relief of the embassy in Baghdad. Protesting that this would not be possible with the supply resources at his disposal, Wavell ordered the despatch of a further transport company from Egypt – 3 Reserve Motor Transport Company, Royal Army Service Corps – to support Habforce.

The task required of Habforce was daunting. It had to travel some 460 miles further east from the railhead at Mafraq in Transjordan to Baghdad. One hundred and twenty-two miles along this journey lay H4, the Iraq Petroleum Company's pumping station, 30 miles from the Iraqi border. The tarmac ended 45 miles after H4. Sixty miles further on from the frontier was Rutbah Fort. Between H4 and Rutbah lay H3, ten miles over the Iraqi border. Rutbah had significant value as a source of water and an airfield. From Rutbah the traveller faced another 220 miles of desolation on an ill-defined track across the desert to Ramadi and thence to Habbaniya. For the first 300 miles of the journey from Mafraq the ground remained at a height of some 1,640 feet above sea level, the first third of which comprised a rough lava-belt plain, after which the ground reverted to undulating stone and sand. At the end of the plateau the ground fell for a

Morris trucks of the Household Cavalry Regiment on the Lava Belt in Transjordan in May 1941 en route to H4. (Col Humphrey Wyndham)

Jewish trucks hired, with their drivers, for Habforce. (Col Humphrey Wyndham)

final 100 miles into the Euphrates valley. Only a march on a compass bearing could guarantee that a traveller unused to the vagaries of direction-finding in the desert would be able to make sense of the mass of tracks, ancient and modern, animal and man-made, that criss-crossed the desert floor, providing danger for the unwary.

In a remarkably short time Habforce was gathered together for war, preparations being made at a furious pace. Whilst the troops had enough vehicles to transport themselves, those required to carry supplies had to be requisitioned in Palestine, most of which also retained their civilian drivers. Every kind of vehicle could be found in the column, from flatbed trucks to buses taken from the streets of Haifa and Jerusalem. Habforce collected itself at Beit Lid on 9 May, familiarizing itself with its new equipment and sorting out orders of march, moving and settling supplies into the various vehicles, and preparing the thousand and one things needed to get the operation on its way. This task was made immeasurably more difficult by reason of the poor state of most of the vehicles inherited or acquired by Habforce, and huge efforts were expended over the coming weeks to keep the show on the road. Water was a particular problem. One gallon per man per day and one gallon per vehicle per day was carried on the trucks, as were seven days' rations on the supply trucks together with a further three days' rations in each fighting vehicle. Strict water discipline was applied: water was only to be drunk at halts, by order of an officer. That said, the quality of the water defied drinking. Some of it was brought from Egypt, and varied in consistency from black to purple, and it required settling for ten minutes before the top part could be drunk.

Members of the Iraqi Desert Police, a force with whom Glubb had himself worked in the past, had recently seized Rutbah Fort and reportedly had been joined by the Arab guerrilla leader Fawzi el-Qawujki, long a thorn in the side of governments of Palestine and Transjordan. These elements had in fact fired the opening shots in the war when they attacked a British road survey party on 1 May. The European staff at the pumping stations had fled and local Bedouin had looted the buildings. Instructed by Clark to seize the fort, the mechanized squadron of the TJFF, based at H4, refused, and were promptly marched back to H3 and disarmed. They had been persuaded that their terms of engagement did not extend to operations outside Transjordan, especially those against their brothers in Iraq. At this inauspicious start Clark decided to divide Habforce into two parts, despatching a flying column ('Kingcol') under Brig Kingstone and ordering it to make best haste to H4 to make contact with Glubb's Arab Legion, before proceeding to capture Rutbah. Kingcol comprised the Headquarters 4 Cavalry Brigade, the Household Cavalry Regiment and Cassano's eight Fordson armoured cars. To these forces were added the battery of 25pdr field guns, A and D Companies and two bren gun carriers of the Essex Regiment under the command of Maj K.F. May, which drove all the way from Haifa in Palestine to Mafraq on 11 May, an independent anti-tank troop with 2pdr guns and the section of 166 Field Ambulance.

With some 2,000 men and 500 vehicles, Kingcol took with it four days' worth of water and five of fuel. On 11 May the move from Beit Lid began, Kingcol leading Habforce across the wide, open clay-covered plain of Esdraelon into the Jordan valley, and thence over the Jordan river and onto the rugged and inhospitable country of the Transjordan plateau. The column stretched for seven miles. That first night was

THE LUFTWAFFE ATTACK ON KINGCOL, 17 MAY 1941
A tired and extended column of vehicles, leading the
advance of Kingcol on the cross-desert march to relieve
RAF Habbaniya, was caught in the open by three low-flying
Messerschmitt Bf.110 twin-engined fighters (1) during
17 May 1941. Diving out of the sun, these aircraft, operating
out of Mosul far to the north, came as an unwelcome
reminder to Brig 'Joe' Kingstone, commander of the
4th Cavalry Brigade around which Kingcol was loosely
based, of the vulnerability of his weak force. German
aircraft had appeared seemingly out of nowhere on 12 May,
dropping bombs on vehicles of 1 Essex, and the prospect
that his force would be attacked decisively from the air was
high. Kingcol was struggling to reach RAF Habbaniya, having
become caught up in soft sand the day before and running
short of water. Vehicles of both the Household Cavalry
Regiment and of the Arab Legion were caught up in the
attack, some miles to the south west of Lake Habbaniya.
The armoured car (2) was a home-made vehicle built for the
Arab Legion by a company in Haifa, whilst the trucks were
15cwt Morris (3) and Chevrolets (4). The HCR had only

recently exchanged their horses for trucks, and few soldiers
had been taught to drive. They were now finding their way
through the vastness of the Iraqi desert under constant
threat of attack from guerrillas and from the air. Fortunately
the Luftwaffe found Kingcol on the move, and not sunk
up to its axles in sand as it had been the day before. The
Bf.110s flew with their German insignia hastily painted
out and Iraqi markings painted in, although other German
markings, most notably the shark's teeth, remained
unchanged. Despite the overwhelming odds, the column
returned a spirited fire with the meagre weapons at their
disposal, namely ancient (and poorly functioning) Hotchkiss
machine-guns (5) and Lewis Guns on anti-aircraft mounts
in the back of the vehicles. One Arab legionnaire, bravely
remaining at his machine-gun and unflinchingly engaging
each attacking aircraft, was mortally wounded. Four
cavalrymen were also wounded as their Morris truck was
destroyed. In the event, although dramatic for those
involved, the Germans were unable to prevent Kingcol's
2,000 men and 500 vehicles from safely arriving at RAF
Habbaniya on 18 May.

RAF bombs falling on Rutbah Wells Fort on 9 May 1941, and apparently missing their target. Glubb's force was hidden to the south, observing the action from the safety of the sand dunes. The bombing was largely ineffective, and Iraqi rifle fire brought down one Blenheim, killing the crew. (IWM CM822)

spent at Mafraq, each unit positioning itself in all-round defence and digging into the stony ground as a precaution against air attack. A large square was formed in the desert, in the centre of which were the ambulances and field hospital, as well as the column headquarters and Royal Signals troop. The Field Artillery positioned themselves facing outwards on the perimeter whilst the RAF armoured cars placed themselves at various points of the compass a mile or two outside the perimeter to warn of attack.

On 9 May RAF Blenheim IVF long-range fighters from 203 Squadron, flying from H4, attacked Rutbah Wells Fort. The Arab Legion, armed only with 1915-vintage Lewis and Hotchkiss guns and unable themselves to force the surrender of the fort, waited expectantly in the desert for the fort's surrender. They were disappointed to see the defenders spiritedly attempting to drive off the aircraft with their rifles, and succeeding in shooting down a Blenheim in the process and killing the crew. Glubb was forced to withdraw to H3 on 9 May whilst Baghdad triumphantly announced that he had been killed. Rather prematurely, his obituary was published in London. On the night of 10 May, however, following the arrival of Cassano's armoured cars, the fort was found abandoned and the way to Habbaniya open.

Kingcol left Mafraq in Transjordan early on the morning of 12 May, arriving at H4, eight hours later. The force bivouacked in the desert some miles further on from the pumping station as a precaution against air attack. Later the following day the march was resumed, the objective being Rutbah Fort, which was reached by the early hours of 14 May. Kingstone had gone on ahead of the main force to meet up with Glubb Pasha, whose Arab Legionnaires had occupied the fort after the Iraqi police had hurriedly vacated it. Now that Rutbah had been taken, Kingcol's task was to race across the desert to reach Habbaniya at the quickest speed. Leaving the fort on 15 May, Kingcol's first objective was Kilo 25, a point on the Baghdad road some 14 miles west of Ramadi, on the Euphrates, to where a brigade of Iraqi troops had been deployed. It

An RAF Fordson armoured car entering Rutbah Wells Fort on 16 May 1941. This photograph was posed for the camera, the Iraqi police having withdrawn from the fort five days previous. (IWM E2943E)

was expected that the 220 miles to Habbaniya would be crossed in two days of driving. On the advice of Col Roberts in Habbaniya, the column was to turn south-east at Kilo 25, thus avoiding a confrontation with the Iraqi brigade at Ramadi, so as to skirt underneath Lake Habbaniya and advance on the cantonment across the bridge at Mujara village. The village had been occupied on 10 May and work begun on a temporary bridge over the water regulator, work that was completed on 16 May.

At 7.50 a.m. on 12 May, with Kingcol spread like locusts on the plain, the column was attacked by a high flying aircraft, bombs showering the trucks of 1 Essex with smoke and sand but making no impact other than announcing that Habforce had been discovered. The aeroplane that carried out the attack dropped its bombs and fired its machine-guns from such a height that the aircraft was assumed by many to be an Iraqi Blenheim. But the Royal Iraq Air Force had no Blenheims. In fact the offending aircraft was a Heinkel 111 of the newly arrived *Fliegerführer Irak*, flying out of Mosul. The day before, just as the air threat to the garrison at Habbaniya appeared to be diminishing, an RAF Blenheim pilot, on patrol in the area of Mosul, was surprised to find himself being attacked by a German Me110 fighter from the same Luftwaffe stable.

Having safely navigated the column to Kilo 25 on 16 May, the column turned off the main route. Disaster then struck, as the inexperienced drivers took their vehicles into the gullies between the sand dunes and hit soft sand. The whole column halted, many of the trucks wallowing in sand up to their axles. Much of that day was spent in recovering vehicles in temperatures of some 120° Fahrenheit. Fortunately the Messerschmitts did not find them and exploit their embarrassment. Having sent the knowledgeable Arab Legion off on a reconnaissance to the north, Kingstone faced the prospect of failure so close to his objective, as supplies of water were by now dangerously low. On their return from the reconnaissance to the north, Glubb's men successfully reconnoitred another route and the column eventually made it at the end of the following day through Mujara. On this day the column was attacked by

RAF Fordson armoured car of No. 2 Armoured Car Squadron RAF at Rutbah Wells Fort. These were based on the Rolls Royce Silver Spirit cars which had been in the Middle East since 1915, although the Fordsons were a more modern variant. The original armoured car weighed 4.2 tonnes, was powered by a 6 cylinder petrol engine and had a crew of three. A steel super-structure was built on the standard Silver Spirit (sometimes called 'Silver Ghost') chassis, with a revolving turret on top, which carried a Vickers heavy machine-gun. By 1939, of the 150 cars in service, over half were in the Middle East or India, although the campaigns of 1941 proved to be their swansong. Before they were withdrawn the cars were fitted with an open-topped turret and re-armed with the Boys anti-tank rifle to provide additional firepower, with a Lewis light machine-gun on the top of the turret. The armoured cars of No. 1 Armoured Car Squadron RAF at RAF Habbaniya were the 1915-vintage Rolls Royce Silver Spirits with Vickers HMGs. (IWM E2957E)

three Bf.110Cs, which struck vehicles of the Arab Legion and the Household Cavalry, killing one Legionnaire and wounding four cavalrymen. Soon after Mujara had been passed, the vanguard of the column reached an outpost eight miles south of the cantonment manned by soldiers of the King's Own. Kingcol had arrived. Although the siege had long since been lifted, Kingcol's march was a feat of historic significance. Glubb, who knew the desert better than most, described it as 'one of the most remarkable examples of military daring in history.'

THE ARRIVAL OF THE LUFTWAFFE

The arrival of German aircraft in Iraqi skies on 14 and 15 May was the direct result of fevered consultations between Baghdad and Berlin in the days following Smart's pre-emptive strikes on the forces occupying the high ground above Habbaniya. With the impending invasion of Russia, however, the resources Germany was able to allocate to operations in Iraq were severely limited. On 3 May, Germany's Foreign Minister, Joachim von Ribbentrop, persuaded Hitler that Dr Fritz Grobba (under the pseudonym of Franz Gehrcke) be secretly returned to Iraq to head up a new mission charged with channelling support to the Rashid Ali regime. Then, on 6 May, Luftwaffe Colonel Werner Junck received instructions in Berlin that he was to take a small force of aircraft to Iraq, operating under Iraqi markings out of Mosul, some 240 miles north of Baghdad. *Fliegerführer Irak* was to comprise a squadron (12 aircraft) of Messerschmitt 110s and one squadron, also of 12 aircraft, of Heinkel 111s. To help him get his force to northern Iraq he was lent some 13 Junkers 52 and 90 transport aircraft, all but three of which were to return to Greece immediately to prepare for the invasion of Crete. Junck was accompanied by Major Axel von Blomberg, whose task was to integrate the *Fliegerführer* with Iraqi forces in operations against the British. The British quickly discovered these arrangements through the Italian diplomatic cipher.

On the same day Berlin arrived at an agreement with the Vichy regime in France that allowed the French colonial administration in Damascus to recover 25 per cent of the weaponry impounded under the terms of surrender in July 1940 in exchange for turning over the

Morris trucks of Habforce making heavy weather of the desert sands. (NAM 48/5710-8)

remainder to Iraqi use. The 'Paris Protocols' allowed Germany and Italy, amongst other things, full landing and provisioning rights in Syria, the right to establish a Luftwaffe base at Aleppo, permission to use ports, roads and railways for transport of equipment to Iraq and to train Iraqi soldiers in Syria with French weapons. Simultaneously Germany despatched an envoy with specific responsibility for despatching French war stores by train to Iraq. In this he was very successful, the first trainload arriving in Mosul via Turkey on 13 May. This included 15,500 rifles with six million rounds of ammunition, 200 machine-guns with 900 belts of ammunition and four 75mm field guns together with 10,000 shells. Two further consignments reached Iraq on 26 and 28 May. In addition to the weaponry transported on 13 May, the French shipped eight 155mm field guns together with 6,000 shells, 354 machine pistols, 30,000 grenades and 32 trucks.

A Luftwaffe Junkers Ju.90 in Iraqi insignia, probably at a Syrian airfield en route to Iraq, May 1941. (Bundesarchiv)

Dr Grobba and his mission reached Aleppo on 9 May and Baghdad on 11 May, accompanied by two Bf.110C fighter aircraft. The bulk of Junck's force arrived in Mosul on 13 May after a flight that had taken them some 1,200 miles in 36 hours. Over the following days these aircraft became increasingly frequent visitors to Baghdad. On 14 May Junck's transport aircraft began staging through Aleppo to Mosul, and a further three He.111 bombers and three Bf.110C fighters arrived in Mosul, two over-laden He.111 aircraft having been left with damaged rear wheels at Palmyra in central Syria. These aircraft were then attacked by roving British fighters and disabled on the rough runway of the airfield. Junck himself arrived in Mosul on 15 May with a further nine aircraft. At the time he knew that Habforce was on its way to Habbaniya, and knew that Kingcol had taken Rutbah Fort on 11 May. So as to be seen by his Iraqi hosts to make an immediate impact, he despatched a lone Heinkel to find Kingcol at Rutbah, successfully

A Heinkel III destroyed at Palmyra airfield, Syria. The swastika on the tail and fuselage can be seen clearly painted out and replaced with Iraqi insignia. (IWM E4076)

Smoke billowing from hangars at RAF Habbaniya following a heavy strike by three Luftwaffe Heinkel III bombers, flying from Mosul some 240 miles to the north, on 16 May 1941. (IWM E3326)

bombing the column and alerting the British to the reality of German military assistance to the Iraqi regime.

On the same day Junck sent von Blomberg to Baghdad to make arrangements for a council of war with the Iraqi Government planned for 17 May. However, an Iraqi soldier guarding a bridge in Baghdad, not recognizing the shape and silhouette of the He.111, and believing it to be British, placed a few well-aimed rounds into the fuselage as it cruised low overhead, making its way to the airport. One of those stray rounds killed von Blomberg instantly, although the aircraft made a safe landing at the civil airfield on the eastern edge of the suburbs.

By the end of that day Junck had assembled a force in northern Iraq comprising five He.111 bombers, 12 Bf.110C fighters, a communications flight with light aircraft, a section of anti-aircraft cannon and three JU.52 transports. Junck himself visited Baghdad on 16 May in place of von

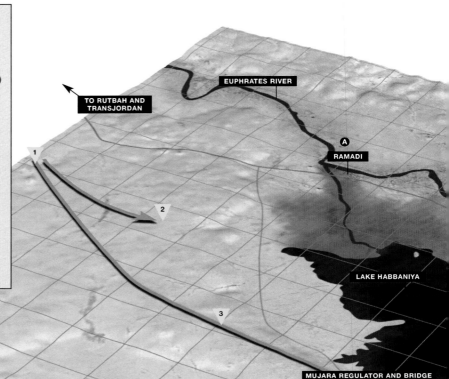

BRITISH UNITS
1. 1 King's Own Royal Regiment (KORR) (forward pickett)
2. 'G' column 1 Company Arab Levies
3. 'A' column (composite levies and 2/4 Gurkha)
4. 'L' column (composite levies and 2/4 Gurkha)
5. 1 King's Own Royal Regiment (KORR) (withdrawn into Falluja 19 May)
6. 'V' column
7. A Company King's Own Royal Regiment (KORR)
8. C Company King's Own Royal Regiment (KORR)
9. Arab Levies
10. A Company 1 Essex
11. D Company 1 Essex
12. C Company Household Cavalry Regiment (HCR)

IRAQI UNITS
A. Iraqi brigade
B. Iraqi brigade destroyed at Habbaniya
C. Remnants of Iraqi brigade destroyed at Habbaniya
D. 6 Infantry Brigade

▼ EVENTS

1. The 'flying column' of Habforce ('Kingcol') moved south of the main track to Ramadi at Kilo 25, during 15 May, and bivouacked alongside the track that would take them round the south of Lake Habbaniya, across the Mujara Bridge. This route would ensure that the force would avoid any confrontation with the Iraqi brigade at Ramadi.

2. On 16 May, however, with no Arab Legion guides to help them, the leading trucks of Kingcol became stuck in sand. It took a whole day to recover the vehicles back to solid ground. A disaster was only averted by the absence that day of Luftwaffe aircraft in the skies.

3. Three Bf.110 twin-engined Luftwaffe fighters found the column, moving carefully towards Mujara on the following day, and attacked at low level. One Arab Legionnaire and four cavalrymen were wounded, and some vehicles destroyed.

4. By the end of the day the first of Kingcol's 2,000 weary troops and dusty vehicles passed the Kings Own Royal Regiment picket at the Mujara Bridge and made their way to RAF Habbaniya.

5. By 18 May the whole of Brig Kingstone's force was complete at RAF Habbaniya, although the remainder of Habforce was to straggle in over the following week-and-a-half. The arrival of Kingcol was the first substantial reinforcement to reach RAF Habbaniya since the collapse of the Iraqi siege on 7 May. It provided a critical enhancement to Col Roberts' forces, which enabled him to launch his attack on the Iraqi-held town of Falluja, the first step on the route to Baghdad, on the following day.

6. The attack on Falluja was a carefully prepared affair comprising four main elements. The first was the insertion of a mixed company-level force of 2/4 Gurkha Rifles and Arab Levies ('L' Column) at the Notch Fall regulator, during the night of 18 May. They crossed the Euphrates at night via the rope bridge at Sin-el-Dhibban. The task of this force was to open up an evacuation route for the troops attacking Falluja if they needed to withdraw.

7. Second, a company of 1 KORR were landed on the desert floor by aircraft astride the road to Baghdad. Their task was to act as a block to any Iraqi troops attempting to reinforce the town.

8. Third, a further mixed column of 2/4 Gurkhas and Arab Levies made its way to the west of Falluja during the night of 18 May. Like 'L' Column, they crossed the Euphrates at Sin-el-Dhibban.

9. The main attack on Falluja was undertaken by an Arab Levie company under the command of Capt Alastair Graham, supported by 3.7-inch howitzers captured from the Iraqis earlier in the fighting, and RAF Rolls Royce armoured cars precariously transported across the raging gap in Hammond's Bund by improvised ferry. Heavy air attacks took place during 19 May, and in the afternoon, under heavy artillery, machine-gun and aerial bombardment, the Levies assaulted the bridge, captured it, and then proceeded to secure the town at no loss to themselves. It was a remarkable achievement.

10. Once Falluja had been captured, however, the British became complacent and did little to defend the town from counter-attack. The Iraqi 6th Infantry Brigade from Baghdad attacked the weak British positions on 22 May, penetrating the town with tanks. It was touch-and-go for some hours as to whether the British would retain hold of the town. However, rapid reinforcement by troops of the Household Cavalry Regiment and 1 Essex, together with the presence on the ground of Brig Kingstone, disaster was averted and the Iraqi attack repelled.

HABBANIYA AND FALLUJA 16-22 MAY 1941

The arrival of the first elements of Habforce at Habbaniya on 16 May heralded a change of fortune for British forces in the region and provided the basis for the subsequent advances on both Falluja and Baghdad.

Note: Gridlines are shown at intervals of 5 Kilometres

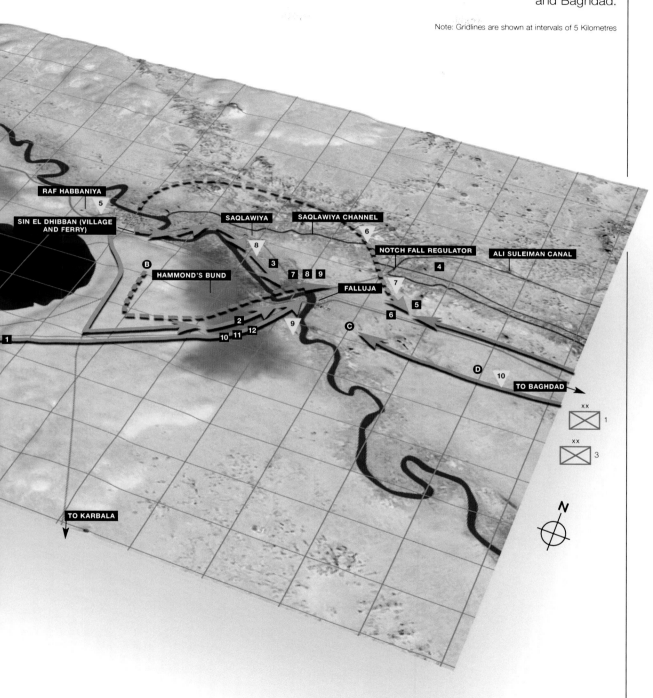

RAF HABBANIYA
5

SIN EL DHIBBAN (VILLAGE AND FERRY)

SAQLAWIYA

SAQLAWIYA CHANNEL
6

NOTCH FALL REGULATOR

ALI SULEIMAN CANAL

B

HAMMOND'S BUND

8

3

7 8 9

4

7

FALLUJA

5

6

1

2

10 11 12

9

C

D

10

TO BAGHDAD

XX
1

XX
3

TO KARBALA

N

Blomberg and held a meeting with Dr Grobba, Rashid Ali, General Amin Zaki, Col Nur ed-Din Mahmud and Mahmud Salman. They agreed a number of immediate priorities for *Fliegerführer Irak*. The first was to prevent Kingcol arriving to succour Habbaniya. The second was to capture Habbaniya itself, it being tacitly assumed by Junck that the Iraqi Army would make the actual assault whilst the Germans provided air cover. The overall aim was to provide what the Germans tellingly described as 'spine straightening' for the Iraqi army, much of which had become terrified of bombing by British aircraft.

Junck decided to launch a surprise attack that very day on Habbaniya, deploying six Bf.110C fighters and three He.111 bombers for the task. The attack took the base by surprise, killing a number on the ground and shooting down two RAF aircraft, an Audax and a Gladiator, the raiders losing a Heinkel in exchange.

Shocked but undaunted, the little Habbaniya air force took the air war to the newly arrived Luftwaffe. On 17 May RAF aircraft reinforcements arrived unannounced from Egypt in the form of four more Gladiators from 94 Squadron and six Blenheim bombers from 84 Squadron. Although the nine remaining Wellingtons in Basra had been withdrawn to Egypt on 12 May to assist in the war against Rommel, two new long-range cannon-firing Hurricanes had also arrived from Aboukir in Egypt. Together with the Blenheims, they made a daring, long-range sortie to hit back at the Luftwaffe at Mosul on 17 May, destroying two and damaging four aircraft for the loss of a Hurricane. On the same day two Gladiators from Habbaniya, loitering around Rashid Airfield at Baghdad, encountered two Bf.110Cs attempting to take off, and destroyed them both, much to the joy of the two British sergeant pilots responsible. Thus within two days of arrival and despite the surprise attack on Habbaniya on 16 May, Junck's force had been whittled down to four He.111 bombers, eight Bf.110C fighters and two JU.52 transport aircraft, a loss of 30 per cent. This rate of attrition did not augur well for the continuance of a strong Luftwaffe presence in Iraq. Indeed, by the end of May Junck had lost 14 Bf.110Cs and five He.111s, an overall loss of 95 per cent of his original fighter and bomber strength. With few replacements available, no spares, poor quality fuel and aggressive attacks by the RAF out of Habbaniya, the mathematics of attrition went in only one direction, and the eventual withdrawal of the Luftwaffe in these circumstances became inevitable.

THE BATTLES FOR FALLUJA AND BAGHDAD

In the week following the end of the Iraqi investment of Habbaniya, Col Ouvry Roberts, the *de facto* commander of the Habbaniya garrison, now grouped together with the infantry reinforcements from Basra (2/4 Gurkha) and from Kingcol (1 Essex) into the 'Habbaniya Brigade', took control of ground operations, putting plans together to attack the town of Falluja as the first stage in striking out in the direction of Baghdad. He dismissed the idea of attacking Ramadi, as it was still garrisoned heavily by the Iraqi army, was largely cut off by self-imposed flooding and could be isolated in favour of securing the strategically important crossing over the Euphrates at Falluja. Success at RAF Habbaniya had provided the British with the initiative for the moment, and it was critical that this momentum be maintained. Delay would allow the Iraqi armed forces time to recover from their recent embarrassment and give the Luftwaffe valuable time to build up its forces in the north. Roberts had wanted to attack much sooner but he was forced to wait until the arrival of Kingcol and its precious artillery, amongst other things. Accordingly, the attack was planned for 19 May.

Both AVM John D'Albiac and MajGen George Clark arrived by air in Habbaniya on 18 May. Clark agreed to leave Roberts to carry out his operation without interference. Falluja sits astride the Euphrates river. Its 177-foot long iron bridge was a key strategic feature, linking Habbaniya with Baghdad only 30 miles further on. However, most of the western approaches to Falluja and its precious bridge were all under water for a distance of some four miles, a consequence of the deliberate flooding by the Iraqis of the low-lying areas under the Euphrates'

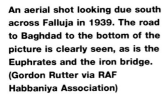

An aerial shot looking due south across Falluja in 1939. The road to Baghdad to the bottom of the picture is clearly seen, as is the Euphrates and the iron bridge. (Gordon Rutter via RAF Habbaniya Association)

THE ATTACK ON FALLUJA, 19 MAY 1941

A company of the Iraq Levies (1), under the command of Captain Alistair Graham of the Green Howards, launched an attack on the strategically vital Falluja Bridge in the early afternoon of 19 May. The capture of this bridge was vital in the campaign, as it provided the only crossing of the Euphrates for many miles and lay directly on the route to Baghdad. Graham's company had crossed the flooded Hammond's Bund during the previous night and had taken up defensive positions some way short of the bridge during the morning. The Iraqi Levies, fiercely loyal to Great Britain, proved themselves to be more than the equal of the regular troops of the Iraqi Army, although trained merely to guard the air base and cantonment at RAF Habbaniya and RAF Shaibah, near Basra. During this attack the Levies wore British steel helmets, 1938-pattern webbing and khaki overalls. They were also supported by 3.7in howitzers, small, highly manoeuvrable weapons that had also been transported across the bund. The bridge was captured by the Levies without a single casualty and the troops then rushed in to seize the town. Iraqi troops surrendered, fled or melted into the civilian populace by shedding their uniforms. Many were recognized, however, by the fact that they were loath to discard their army boots. The attack on Falluja was planned by Colonel Ouvry Roberts, chief staff officer (GSO1) to the 10 Indian Division then gathering in Basra. Roberts had been caught at RAF Habbaniya at the start of the siege in early May, and had remained there to command the defence of the base and cantonment. Other British forces had been moved during the night to surround and cut off Falluja from all points of the compass. During the morning the assorted aircraft from RAF Habbaniya, including Oxford trainers (2), Blenheim fighter-bombers (3) and ancient Hawker Audaxes (4), carried out a heavy attack, dropping several tons of bombs, and throwing up a dense thrall of smoke and dust over the town. This bombing had been interspersed with drops of leaflets urging the Iraqis to surrender. The combination of psychological and physical attack worked wonders to diminish the resolve of the Iraqi defenders. By this time in the war, the Iraqi Air Force had been largely destroyed, although a considerable threat remained from the recently arrived Luftwaffe. By a stroke of good fortune, however, the Germans did not interfere with the British attacks on Falluja. If they had done so it would have seriously diminished the effect of the British bombing, given hope to the beleaguered Iraqi defenders and interfered with Graham's ground assault. The final assault by the Arab Levies was supported by the Vickers machine-guns of a small number of First World War-era Rolls Royce armoured cars (5). These had been transported, with considerable difficulty, across the gap in Hammond's Bund the previous night, perched precariously on hastily prepared pontoons. Although ancient, these vehicles proved to be of considerable worth during the campaign, providing a modicum of armoured mobility to a force otherwise bereft of armoured protection. Whilst some had been part of the inventory of RAF Habbaniya for decades, others had made the long journey from Egypt in the company of Kingcol.

Falluja Bridge, snapped by Pte Jimmy Glass, a driver in 552nd Transport Company, Royal Army Service Corps, from the top of a Morris 15cwt truck in early June 1941. (Jim Glass)

Arab Levies guarding the vital iron bridge over the Euphrates at Falluja following its capture on 19 May 1941. (Col Humphrey Wyndham)

'bunds'. The incomplete Mujara–Falluja road (Hammond's Bund) had been cut in half by Iraqi demolitions and a roaring torrent flowed through the gap, resisting all but the most serious attempts to cross it. This limited the options available to Roberts as he contemplated how best to secure the bridge without its first being destroyed. He had none of the traditional bridge-building or water-crossing equipment he might have expected, and limited artillery support to cover the crossings. Likewise the crossing at Sin-el-Dhibban had very limited capacity. The flooding made a traditional ground assault out of the question, and surprise was essential to prevent the Iraqis blowing up the bridge. Roberts was keen to ensure that street fighting in the town should be avoided at all costs, in part because of the limited numbers of his troops but also because the town would be crowded with civilians. A different approach was therefore required.

The plan he came up with was one of brilliant improvisation. He envisaged an attack with two phases. In the first he intended to shower the Iraqi defenders with leaflets encouraging them to surrender before they were swallowed up by the vast (albeit imaginary) British army advancing from the west and the south, that same army that had so decisively bettered the forces on the plateau at Habbaniya two weeks before. This attack would be preceded by an early morning aerial bombardment. He would follow up this leaflet raid with a heavy aerial strike on the town, in an effort to reason with the defenders both physically and psychologically. At the same time he would cut off the town from telegraphic contact with Baghdad. This would be achieved by the simple but dangerous expedient of flying Audaxes through the telephone lines. Where there was more than one line, the pilot would land and cut the wires by hand whilst his passenger chopped down the pole.

Air attacks were to be fully co-ordinated with land operations in the advance out of Habbaniya. GrpCapt Casey had taken responsibility for air operations alongside Roberts, and the two dimensions had for some time now been fully integrated.

The second phase of Roberts' plan was a three-pronged assault on Falluja, the primary objective of which was to secure the bridge. If the Iraqis failed to heed the written warnings dropped by leaflet, or were insufficiently cowed by his aerial and artillery bombardment, his small force would launch an attack to secure the bridge and the town. One column with about 100 Levies under the command of Capt Alistair Graham would advance along Hammond's Bund and cross the gap by improvised ferry, rushing the bridge at dawn on 19 May. At the same time three columns of Levies and 2/4 Gurkhas with RAF armoured cars and captured 3.7in howitzers would cross the Euphrates at Sin-el-Dhibban (where the Iraqis had previously used a ferry) and then threaten Falluja from the north-west, establishing positions in the area of Notch Falls astride the road leading from Falluja to Ramadi. Their task was to attack Falluja from the west, and to prevent the town from being reinforced by the brigade at Ramadi, although the extensive flooding prevented this force drawing in to the outskirts of the town. The river at Sin-el-Dhibban was 750 feet wide with a strong current, and the Madras Sappers and Miners brought up from Basra to build a ferry did so with 1,500 feet of wire hawser. Further south, a wide assortment of pleasure boats from Lake Habbaniya had been brought up to cross the flooded breach at Hammond's Bund. The Levies had prepared for this moment by practising on Yacht Club boats in the Habbaniya swimming pool. In the third phase, a company of the King's Own were to be transported by air in a daring airborne manoeuvre to cut the road between Falluja and Baghdad, thus preventing Iraqi reinforcements from assisting the town's defenders.

During the night of 18 May, the Notch Falls column crossed by the raft at Sin-el-Dhibban and approached Falluja from the north-west under cover of darkness. Simultaneously, Captain Graham's Levies also began laboriously crossing the flood gap at Hammond's Bund in the darkness. It took all night to get the troops into position. Air attacks began as planned at 5 a.m. on 19 May for an hour on targets around Falluja involving 57 aircraft, after which leaflets were dropped on the town urging the defenders to surrender. Roberts' aim was to give the

Communicating in the desert. Radios were non-existent and armoured cars were forced to rely on semaphore, a throw-back to the days when the armoured cars were part of the Royal Navy. (G. Rutter via RAF Habbaniya Association)

Iraqi defenders time to surrender or escape. In the early dawn light the company of the King's Own were flown by four Valentia aircraft to a position on the Baghdad road two miles north-east of Falluja, landing on the desert floor. The aircraft landed blind on the desert and took a matter of minutes only to disgorge their occupants before taking off again for the safety of Habbaniya.

Roberts hoped that artillery and air pressure, together with the knowledge that they were surrounded, would persuade the defenders to melt away. After a break during the morning a short but ferocious dive-bombing attack took place on Falluja at 2.45 p.m., followed by a rush on the Falluja Bridge by Graham's Levies, supported by artillery fire from the troop of 3.7in howitzers, as well as machine-guns and mortars. The bridge and the town were successfully secured and some 300 enemy prisoners captured. The RAF had thrown nearly ten tons of bombs at the town in 134 sorties, and when the Levies attacked they suffered not a single casualty: the enemy had melted away as Roberts had hoped, discarding their uniforms and merging with the civilian population if they could not get out of the town itself. His job over, Roberts returned south to Shaibah to rejoin the 10 Indian Division on 21 May. Graham was awarded a military cross for leading the attack.

The next two days were spent clearing up Falluja and preparing defences to the north of the town. Nothing was seen of the enemy. However, unexpectedly fierce Iraqi counter-attacks were made against Falluja by the Iraqi 6 Infantry Brigade, accompanied by a number of Fiat light tanks, on 22 May. British forces in the town had thinned out already and only a light defensive screen was in position facing the road to Baghdad, comprising A and C Companies of the King's Own, plus a platoon of the Iraq Levies.

The first indication of trouble was a rumble on the road to Baghdad at 2.30 a.m. and what appeared to be a mass of vehicles coming down the road from Baghdad. Lt C.J. Hodgson of the King's Own promptly took out a patrol to investigate and in the process discovered a large Iraqi force preparing to assault the town. With a haversack of grenades he proceeded to attack these troops with no thought for his own safety, and was cut down and killed in the attempt. By 3 a.m. the Iraqis had reached the north-eastern outskirts of the town, where a heavy mortar bombardment covered the forward trenches of C Company of the King's Own and forced the defenders to withdraw amongst the buildings at the edge of the town. Two tanks entered the town but were quickly destroyed and a spirited counter-attack by a platoon from A Company managed to push the Iraqis out of the town by dawn. The commanding officer of the King's Own was wounded by a sniper at this juncture. An attack with infantry and tanks then developed against the south-eastern edge of the town, which was defended by A Company of the King's Own, but the Iraqis made no progress through the stubborn defence in over nine hours of fighting. By 10 a.m. Brig Kingstone had managed to get forward from Habbaniya to take personal command of the defence of Falluja, bringing with him reinforcements in the shape of the two Essex Regiment companies (A and D), and C Squadron of the Household Cavalry. These troops quickly crossed the gap in Hammond's Bund and marched the seven miles into Falluja, carrying anti-tank rifles, Hotchkiss guns and ammunition on their backs, wading neck-deep in some places through the flood waters. Makeshift rafts were built to cross areas that were under water. Thrown directly into the battle when they arrived, A Company of 1 Essex quickly cleared the eastern side of the town, but slowed down considerably in the northern outskirts, where the enemy was well dug-in in trenches, and where light machine-guns positioned on rooftops in the north of the town covered the main roads and approaches. Fighting was fierce, but the Essex companies methodically cleared the Iraqi positions, house-by-house. It was a critical juncture of the battle. However, by 6 p.m. the remaining Iraqi troops had fled or had been taken prisoner, the final snipers had been silenced, and the town was quiet.

The Iraqi 6 Brigade had made a gallant and determined attempt to eject the British from Falluja and had come near to succeeding. Disaster for the British was averted only by the staunchness of the defenders, together with the speed by which reinforcements were able to reach the town from Habbaniya. The King's Own suffered 50 casualties in the fighting, including one officer killed and four wounded, 16 other ranks killed and 25 wounded. Six light tanks were captured and over 100 prisoners, including two officers. Brig Kingstone was awarded an immediate bar to his Distinguished Service Order (DSO) and a DSO, Military Cross and Military Medal were awarded to officers and soldiers of 1 Essex.

The defence of Falluja maintained the offensive momentum of the British advance, and meant that the route to Baghdad remained open. Rather belatedly, the Luftwaffe put in an appearance on 23 May, strafing Falluja with machine-guns on three separate occasions, although they achieved nothing more than nuisance value. Iraqi artillery rather in effectively bombarded Falluja during the day. Despite the attempt on 16 May to co-ordinate the efforts of *Fliegerführer Irak* with Iraqi ground forces none was apparent during this critical battle on 22 May. A co-ordinated assault on the town by both ground and air forces may well have tipped the balance in Iraq's favour even at this stage and recovered the bridge.

During this period Glubb's Arab Legionnaires were dominating the tribal country to the north between the Euphrates and the Tigris, an area known as the 'Jezireh'. Glubb had been instructed to persuade the local tribes to desist in supporting the Baghdad government, and with a combination of propaganda and raids against government posts he proved remarkably successful. The influence of the Arab Legion was such that German propaganda broadcasts continued to claim that 'Colonel Glubb' of the Arab Legion had been killed, a stratagem designed to spread despondency amongst the many tribespeople loyal to the Regent and to persuade them not to support the British forces.

THE BATTLE OF BAGHDAD

The most direct route to Baghdad was from the west along the road from Falluja, but it was also the most obvious and Iraqi defences there were likely to be strong. Another option was to attack from the south and for troops to be diverted through the holy city of Karbala, perhaps linking up with the 10 Indian Division advancing north from Ur. A third alternative was to advance on Baghdad from the north, along the direction of the Mosul road. The plan eventually adopted was chosen in order to maintain the momentum gained by the successful defence of Falluja on 22 May and in the expectation that the Iraqis had no idea about how small and vulnerable Clark's forces actually were. To wait for Slim's division to advance from the south would have added substantial delay to the operation: indeed, 10 Indian Division was only given orders to advance out of Basra on 25 May. Clark decided that in addition to a thrust from the east a strong detachment would cross the desert north-east to cut the Baghdad–Mosul road and railway, Slim would continue to threaten from the south, and the maximum pressure would be exerted from the air.

It was, nevertheless, a high-risk plan. Clark had but some 1,450 men, including about 250 of the Arab Legion: the Iraqi Army had at least 20,000 troops in the Baghdad area, including a brigade to the west at Ramadi, German aircraft were active in the skies above and substantial water obstacles lay between Falluja and the gates of Baghdad. Indeed, two separate patrol actions north and west from Falluja on 24 May proved how tenuous the British position was. D Company of 1 Essex despatched a strong fighting patrol less than a mile to the north of Falluja, encountering a large body of Iraqi troops in the process. The Iraqi unit fought back and, although the Essex patrol inflicted some casualties, they were forced to withdraw. Despite the loss of Habbaniya and Falluja, many Iraqi units, until that time not involved in the fighting, remained full of fight. On the same day a truck-mounted patrol from B Squadron of the Household Cavalry Regiment, together with two RAF armoured cars, took position on the main road west of Ramadi, with the task of preventing the escape of Iraqis from the village and of reporting on the effects of RAF bombing on the Iraqi brigade positions. However, the weakly armed patrol was attacked by upward of 100 Iraqis the next morning, almost certainly irregulars belonging to Fawzi el-Qawujki. To complicate the situation both armoured cars became bogged down in the sand and had to be abandoned. The troop commander, Lt Leigh, accompanied by Lt Wellesley, who had been despatched to assist in the recovery of the armoured cars, were forced to make a hurried withdrawal on 26 May to the west side of Lake Habbaniya

and back to the cantonment the long way across the Mujara Bridge. Only
one of the armoured cars was recovered, the other being captured by Fawzi
and used against the British later in the campaign in the area of
Abu Kemal.

However, Clark judged that if the impetus of operations could be
sustained across the country, both on land and in the air, this plan might
just pay off. After all, bluff and high stakes had already paid off
handsomely at Habbaniya, with Kingcol's advance across the desert and
the capture of Falluja, and there was every reason to expect that they
would be successful again. There was also evidence that support for the
rebel government in many areas was waning. Boldness at the right time
and the maintenance of the momentum gained so far could bring
substantial dividends.

Brig Kingstone took a column directly along the Falluja–Baghdad
Road whilst a column commanded by LtCol Andrew Ferguson of the
Household Cavalry traversed the desert to join the main road to
Baghdad from Mosul in the north at Meshahida. The forces in both
columns were tiny, Kingstone's comprising a squadron of the
Household Cavalry, A and D companies of the Essex Regiment, with
three armoured cars and a troop of 25pdrs, a total of only some
750 men. Ferguson's column boasted A and B Squadrons of the
Household Cavalry Regiment, a troop of 25pdrs, three further RAF
armoured cars and 250 men (16 fighting sections) of Glubb's Arab
Legion, a total of only 700.

The pitifully small Habforce was by now advancing on Baghdad in
what was a dangerous game of bluff. Kingstone made steady progress in

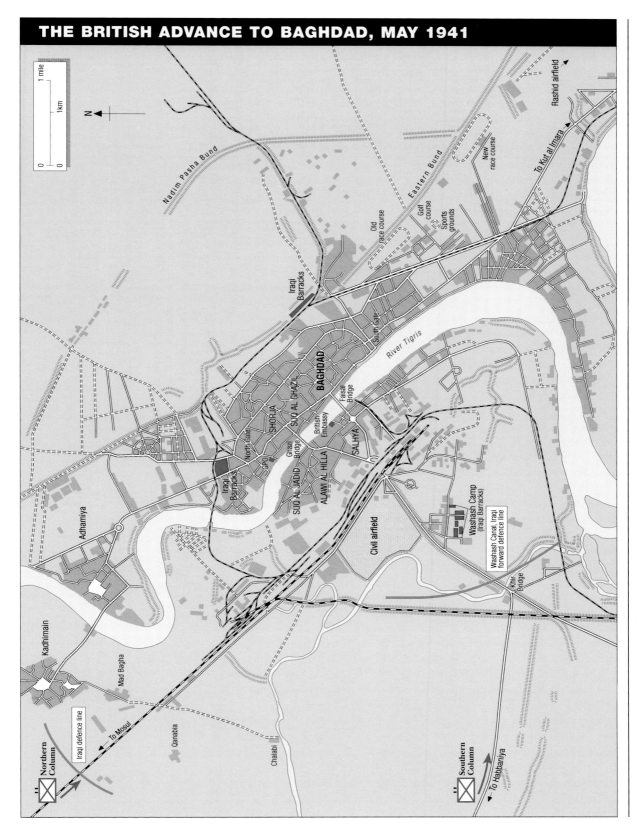

1 mile

1km

N

Rashid airfield

To Kut al Imara

New race course

Eastern Bund

Nadim pasha Bund

Old race course

Golf course

Sports grounds

Iraqi Barracks

South Gate

River Tigris

BAGHDAD

SHORJA

SUQ AL GHAZL

British Embassy

Faisal Bridge

SALHYA

(North Gate)

Ghazi Bridge

GPO

Iraqi Barracks

SUQ AL JADID

ALAWI AL HILLA

Civil airfield

Washash Camp (Iraqi Barracks)

Washash Canal, Iraqi forward defence line

Kifir Bridge

Adhamiya

Kadhimain

Mad Bagha

To Mosul

Qanabia

Chalabi

Northern Column

Iraqi defence line

Southern Column

To Habbaniya

the south during 28 May, leaving Falluja at 4.45 a.m., slowed only by pockets of resistance along the road and by the flooding. The fort at Khan Nuqta 20 miles further on from Falluja was seized after a show of force in which an Iraqi battalion headquarters was captured by a troop of C Squadron of the Household Cavalry Regiment. The column finished the day some 12 miles from Baghdad at the demolished bridge over the Abu Ghuraib canal, although the route had been made extremely difficult by virtue of the wide trenches the Iraqis had cut across the road, and the floodwaters that gushed through the gaps in the bunds. As each impediment was reached the Royal Engineers managed to cross the 20-yard wide breach, but it made the advance frustratingly slow. The Iraqis were well entrenched on the far bank, with numerous machine-gun positions covering both the road and the breach. A and D Companies of 1 Essex could make no immediate headway against this fire, although after several hours' shelling by the 25pdrs an infantry patrol managed to get across the damaged bridge at about 10 a.m. At noon on 29 May elements of Kingstone's column managed to cross the bridge and Iraqi positions in front of Baghdad were pounded by artillery and from the air. Whilst the infantry were able to push forward they did so without their vehicles, which only began to cross during the mid-morning of 30 May after the Royal Engineers had repaired the bridge sufficient to enable it to take wheeled traffic again.

In the north, after crossing the Euphrates at night on 27 May, Glubb's Arab Legion guided the men of Ferguson's column through the desert until they met the Mosul–Baghdad road. Ferguson missed a chance to drive straight into Baghdad on the evening of 27 May, instead bivouacking six miles north of the city that night. Had his small force pressed on it would have undoubtedly managed to seize the city, as they were entirely unexpected, the government being taken by surprise by the advance from the north. A strong Iraqi infantry force prevented their movement the next morning, and the element of surprise was lost. Thereafter, apart from cutting portions of the railway line leading to Mosul north of the railway station at Taji, the column made slow progress against stiff opposition in the brickworks of Al Kadhimain, near one of the holiest sites in Shia Islam. The shell and machine-gun fire was intense and wholly unexpected: indeed, as Lt Gerard Leigh was later to acknowledge, this engagement was the squadron's first uncomfortable baptism of fire. One trooper was killed and five were wounded, and it saw the end of Ferguson's brave attempt to threaten a thrust into Baghdad from the north. For some reason the troop of 25pdrs was not brought forward to assist in this attack. It was simply not possible, with all the dash and verve in the world, for the two truck-borne cavalry squadrons, one machine-gun troop and one 25pdr troop to overcome what was most likely a full enemy brigade extended along positions defending the north-western approaches to Iraq's capital city.

The advance of Clark's force from Falluja was accompanied by the long awaited move north out of the Basra base by the two brigades of Slim's 10 Indian Division, which began on 27 May. The first phase of the move, prior to the advance on Baghdad following the course of both the Euphrates and the Tigris rivers, was the securing of the ancient city of Ur, birthplace of Abraham. This was achieved successfully by Weld's 21 Indian Brigade, which moved north on the afternoon of 28 May. The

A photograph of the Union Flag being raised on the roof of the British Embassy in Baghdad on 1 June 1941. The photograph was snapped by Lt Peter Bindloss of 1 Essex. (Peter Bindloss)

A photograph of the Union Flag being raised on the roof of the British Embassy in Baghdad on 1 June 1941. The photograph was snapped by Lt Peter Bindloss of 1 Essex. (Peter Bindloss)

few opportunistic attacks made on the brigade were dispersed with artillery fire.

While the two Habforce columns were working their way towards the capital, difficult consolidation operations were being undertaken simultaneously from Falluja. Constant patrolling against strong pockets of enemy, and the daily harassment of sniping attacks, made the task extremely difficult. A major engagement against a heavily entrenched Iraqi unit took place on 28 May at the regulator on the Abu Ghuraib Canal and served as a reminder that the campaign was far from over. Two platoons from 1 Essex, together with a machine-gun section of the Levies, were unable to get within half a mile of the Iraqi position, which was held in considerable strength and with well protected flanks. An artillery barrage and air attack on the position during the evening failed to force the Iraqis to withdraw, and was met by heavy machine-gun and artillery fire in response. A number of British casualties were incurred and a withdrawal was ordered. On the following day the RAF attacked the position and an assault by two companies of 1 Essex was prepared. In the event, however, the British artillery fire was poorly observed, and it, together with the air attacks, missed their targets. Insult was added to injury when the RAF showered the 1 Essex companies 'with pamphlets in Iraqi calling upon them to surrender.' Given the self-evident strength of the Iraqi position, which was believed to be held by at least a battalion, common sense prevailed and the infantry assault was called off in the search for a more imaginative plan of attack. In the event the cessation of hostilities two days later removed this necessity entirely.

By this stage of the operation Clark had successfully created a feeling of superiority over the enemy out of all proportion to the size of his force. The impression the advance had created, together with intensive British air activity, was such that Baghdad would soon be surrounded. British troops had managed to cut off the road to Mosul (although there was no appreciation of the extreme weakness of Ferguson's position), the main body of the British force was advancing from Falluja after having successfully crossed 500 miles of desert from Palestine, and the 10 Indian Division in the south had broken out to capture Ur and was

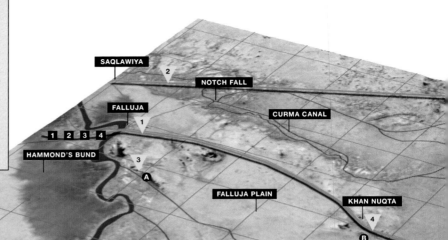

BRITISH UNITS
1 C Squadron Household Cavalry Regiment (HCR)
2 A and D Companies Essex Regiment
3 Three Rolls Royce armoured cars
4 Troop of 25-pounders
5 A and B Squadrons Household Cavalry Regiment (HCR)
6 Troop of 25-pounders
7 Three Rolls Royce armoured cars
8 250 Arab Legionnaires under Glubb Pasha

IRAQI UNITS
A Infantry brigade
B Battalion HQ
C Iraqi brigade

▼ EVENTS

1. **The main advance on Baghdad finally got underway at 0445 hrs on 28 May 1941.** The delay of six days since the Iraqi counter-attack at Falluja had been repelled was necessary because the main body of Habforce did not finally arrive at RAF Habbaniya on their journey across the desert from Palestine until 25 May. Several days were required to transport the armoured cars, trucks and troops across the Euphrates at Sin-el-Dhibban and the gap in Hammond's Bund. As it was, the force sent to Baghdad along the main road running due east was tiny. Commanded by Brig Kingstone himself, it comprised C Squadron of the Household Cavalry, A and D Companies of the Essex Regiment, three Rolls Royce armoured cars, and a troop of 25-pounders. The force was about the size of a battalion: some 750 men, hardly enough to capture a mighty city defended by some 20,000 Iraqi regular troops.

2. **Late the previous evening, on 27 May, a second column, under the command of LtCol Andrew Ferguson, departed across the desert** to the north-east, with instructions to intercept the main Baghdad–Mosul road, and then to approach the capital city from the north. Ferguson's force, likewise, was very weak. It comprised A and B Squadrons of the Household Cavalry, a troop of 25-pounders, three Rolls Royce armoured cars and 250 Arab Legionnaires under Glubb Pasha.

3. **On the morning that Kingstone's column got underway a weak composite company** from 1 Essex and Iraq Levies encountered a strongly entrenched Iraqi battalion dug-in around the regulator on the Abu Ghuraib Canal. The Iraqis refused to budge, despite being attacked from the air and by artillery

that evening. It was testament to the fact that the fighting was far from over, and that substantial elements of the Iraqi Army refused to be cowed by the British.

4. **Kingstone's column nevertheless made rapid progress during the 28th,** reaching the Iraqi-held fort of Khan Nuqta during the morning, and capturing the HQ of an Iraqi battalion. The Iraqi telephone system at the fort remained connected to Baghdad, and an Arabic interpreter with the force contacted the city warning of an advance by 'many' British tanks. It was pure bluff, but it had the effect of demoralizing still further the defending troops, many of whom believed that their armed forces' defeat at both Habbaniya and Falluja denoted the inherent superiority of the British invaders and the inevitability of a British victory.

5. **During the remainder of 28 May** Kingstone's column drove hard and brazenly directly towards Baghdad. The bridges over the canals had been destroyed, and a number of other breaches had been made by the Iraqis in the bunds along which the column travelled. However, the Iraqis had failed to cover their demolitions with artillery or machine-gun fire, with the result that the Royal Engineers with the column were able rapidly to erect temporary bridges that enabled the column to cross and continue its advance.

6. **By the end of the first day, Kingstone had made remarkable progress,** and stood with his lead vehicles at the destroyed bridge over the Abu Ghuraib canal, some 12 miles from the outskirts of Baghdad.

7. **Meanwhile, Ferguson's column to the north** had made good progress, bivouacking a mere six miles to the north of Baghdad on 27 May. The next morning, on 28 May, as Kingstone was setting out from Falluja, Ferguson's column attacked and captured the railway station at Taji. But further advance on Baghdad proved impossible for Ferguson's weak force. On 29 and 30 May, Ferguson tried to push his troops past the brickworks at Al Kadhimain, but the Iraqi defence, comprising probably a whole Iraqi brigade, were too strong to be defeated. Ferguson's pressure form the north, however, was an unwelcome surprise for the Iraqis, and added greatly to the general feeling in Baghdad that the British were in overwhelming strength.

ADVANCE TO BAGHDAD 28-30 MAY 1941

The British advance on Baghdad was to prove a masterful example of bluff as the forces deployed would not have been able to overcome determined opposition. The recent success at Falluja meant that the comparatively small British force threw a long shadow.

Note: Gridlines are shown at intervals of 5 Kilometres

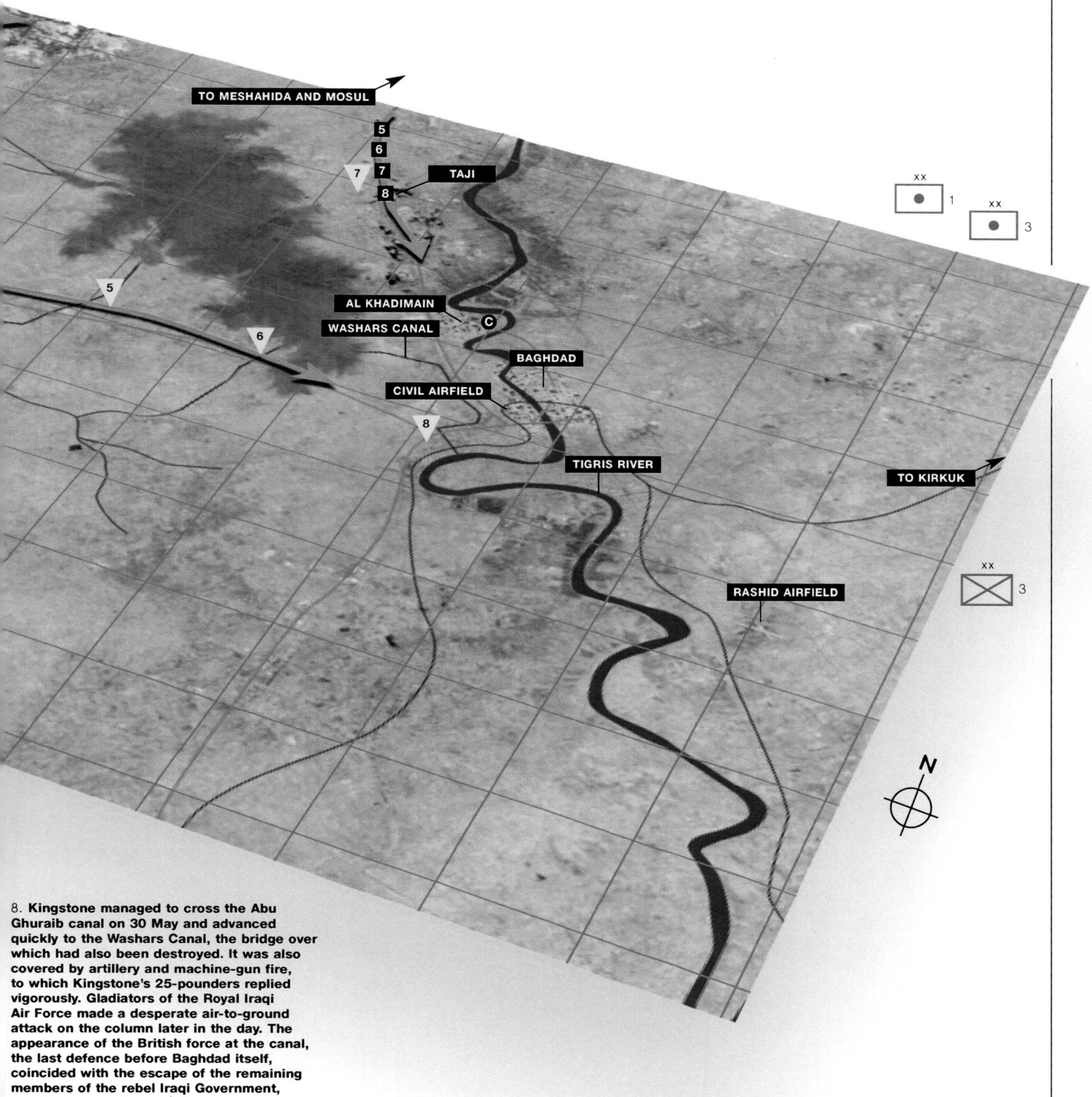

TO MESHAHIDA AND MOSUL

5
6
7
8

TAJI

AL KHADIMAIN
WASHARS CANAL
C
BAGHDAD

CIVIL AIRFIELD

8

TIGRIS RIVER

TO KIRKUK

RASHID AIRFIELD

5

6

XX 1

XX 3

XX 3

N

8. **Kingstone managed to cross the Abu Ghuraib canal on 30 May and advanced quickly to the Washars Canal, the bridge over which had also been destroyed. It was also covered by artillery and machine-gun fire, to which Kingstone's 25-pounders replied vigorously. Gladiators of the Royal Iraqi Air Force made a desperate air-to-ground attack on the column later in the day. The appearance of the British force at the canal, the last defence before Baghdad itself, coincided with the escape of the remaining members of the rebel Iraqi Government, and forced the Mayor to sue for peace. An Armistice was signed between both sides on the banks of the Washars Canal, the next morning, 31 May 1941. Baghdad had fallen.**

making steady progress northwards, despite the hindrances posed by flooding and sporadic defences.

On 28 May Grobba sent a panicked message to Berlin reporting that the British were close to the city with more than 100 tanks, Junck had been reduced to two He.111s with only four bombs and none of his Bf.110Cs were serviceable. In Baghdad wild rumours were spreading about the strength of the British advance. These reports, amongst others, panicked the city and contributed to the final collapse of government, being sufficient to persuade Rashid Ali and a group of 40 others, including the Grand Mufti, to flee under cover of darkness to Iran on the night of 29 May. The Germany military mission to Syria was evacuated and on 30 May Fritz Grobba himself left for Mosul.

A Bren Carrier of 1 Essex at Palmyra on 12 July 1941. It would have made the journey from Palestine to Baghdad, and thence back to take part in the invasion of Syria. (IWM E4089)

After repairing the Abu Ghuraib bridge, Kingstone's column continued its advance on Baghdad on 30 May, the only obstacle between him and Baghdad being now the Washash Canal, which boasted elaborate defences and a well-defended bridge. That afternoon the column's armoured cars came under heavy artillery and machine-gun fire, attacks which were in turn successfully subdued by the counter-fire of Kingstone's 25pdrs. Iraqi Gladiators also managed to strafe A Company of 1 Essex. By now, to all intents and purposes the British had created a stranglehold on the city: what the Iraqi defenders had no means of knowing was just how small Clark's forces were. With Ferguson's column five miles to the north, Kingstone's three miles to the east, incessant air attack and rumours sweeping the city, the mayor of the city approached Cornwallis in the British Embassy to seek terms for surrender at about 8 p.m. that evening.

Early the next morning, 31 May 1941, the mayor led a delegation to meet at the Washash Bridge, together with Sir Kinahan Cornwallis who

Iraqi Army cavalry photographed on the outskirts of Baghdad on 5 June 1941, after the armistice, returning to their barracks. (IWM E3075E)

had been released from his captivity to agree terms. These were quickly agreed. On the basis that the war had been a political contest against Rashid Ali, rather than a war against the Iraqi people, the Iraqi Army was allowed to return to its peacetime locations with all its weapons and equipment, the terms of the Anglo-Iraq Treaty were to be restored, Germans and Italians were to be interned at RAF Habbaniya, prisoners of war on both sides repatriated and the Iraqi garrison in Ramadi evacuated. To the fury of the British and Indian troops who had managed to capture gold-dust-like Bren guns, Bren gun carriers and other equipment from the Iraqi Army, they were ordered to return them to their erstwhile owners. The Household Cavalry were incandescent with rage. They had been forced to divest themselves of their Bren guns before leaving England, had captured a number from the Iraqis in the course of the Euphrates battles, and now, at the end of the armistice, they were forced to hand them back to their defeated foe! Unsurprisingly, many did not. One, a Bren carrier captured at Falluja, rechristened 'Southend-on-Sea' and painted in desert-coloured paint to disguise its giveaway Iraqi Army olive-green, somehow found its way onto the equipment inventory of 1 Essex and completed its war service in the British Army.

AFTERMATH

The Regent returned to Baghdad on 1 June, having waited at Habbaniya for several days in anticipation of the collapse of Rashid Ali's regime. Partly in order to disguise the weakness of Kingstone's force, the decision was made not to occupy Baghdad immediately. Instead, the Regent was to be restored without having to admit by public demonstration that this had been brought about by British force of arms. It was an unfortunate though understandable decision. In the hiatus that followed, Baghdad was torn apart by rioting and looting, long a traditional resort of the Baghdad mob in such times, the violence being channelled against the wealthy and despised Jewish mercantile elite. Some 120 Jews lost their lives and 850 were injured in the violence as the Jewish Quarter was sacked until the otherwise complacent Iraqi police were ordered to restore order with live ammunition.

Mosul was occupied on 3 June and Kirkuk a few days later following an airlift of troops from 2/4 Gurkha Rifles and the King's Own from Habbaniya, joined by the trucks of the Household Cavalry travelling by road. The road group was called 'Gocol' after its commander, Maj R.E.S. Gooch, and comprised B Squadron, six RAF armoured cars, two 3.7in howitzers and RASC transport. Leaving Baghdad on 2 June the column travelled alongside the Tigris northwards for 127 miles before bivouacking near K2 that night. The next day they pushed on the 118 remaining miles to Mosul, which they reached just before noon. The 2/4 Gurkha Rifles were in possession of the airfield, and Gocol was

The returning Regent greeting loyal subjects, Baghdad, 1 June 1941. (IWM E3068E)

Gunners of 237 Battery, 60 Field Regiment Royal Artillery, cleaning their 25pdrs in Baghdad after the armistice. The speed with which Kingstone could bring his 25pdrs to bear against Iraqi defences at Abu Ghuraib and the Washash Canal was an important factor in the collapse of the Iraqi defences. (IWM E3467)

The move of 4/13th FFR from Basra to Kut as part of 21 Indian Brigade in mid-June 1941 (Operation *Regatta*) with the armoured cars of the 13th Lancers. (NAM 144/1965-04-64)

Part of the convoy of 21 Indian Bde on the Tigris en route to Kut in Operation *Regatta*, between 11 and 17 June 1941. The photograph is of the stern-wheeler IHSAN with two barges alongside. The IHSAN carried 500 troops. The photo was taken from the ZENOBIA. On the left can be seen the Iraqi liaison officer, Maj Muzhin, and on the right the British agent in Basra, Mr G. Campbell, who was also a lieutenant in the Royal Navy Reserve. (NA ADM 199/446)

despatched on a mission inside French Syria, in an effort to try to apprehend Dr Grobba, who was thought to have escaped from Mosul and made for the town of Kameschle. Over the week that followed 7 June, Gocol enjoyed a series of adventures that would have done justice to the *Boy's Own* magazine, the column ranging far and wide, and quite illegally, in French territory in pursuit of their quarry. To their great disappointment they reached Kameschle to find that Dr Grobba, perhaps hearing of their approach, had fled.

At the same time a second column had been formed under the commander of Maj E.J.H. Merry, named 'Mercol', which left Habbaniya on the later afternoon of 6 June heading for Haditha, with the task of rounding up gangs of irregular troops working under the authority of Fawzi el-Qawujki. Mercol comprised A Squadron of the Household Cavalry, two RAF armoured cars and the two antique 4.5-inch (18pdr) field

HMS *Cockchafer*, the gunboat to which HM The Regent fled in late April 1941, is aground in the narrows of the Tigris river, being pulled off by the requisitioned Iraqi river steamer *Sumana*, during the advance by river of 21 Indian Brigade to Kut. (NA ADM 199/446)

guns of the Habbaniya arsenal, together with fuel, rations and water for a week. Mercol found Fawzi el-Qawujki's force without difficulty in the area of Abu Kemal, but was surprised to find that the irregulars, numbered around 500, were well armed and possessed some 71 trucks. However, the worth of the antique Habbaniya field guns was proved yet again, and Mercol launched an attack which dispersed Fawzi el-Qawujki's men in haste across the French Syrian border. Unlike Maj Gooch, who had been instructed to pursue Dr Grobba regardless of the international niceties associated with respect for national boundaries, Maj Merry reluctantly broke off the pursuit once the border was reached. These troublesome irregulars were to continue their nuisance attacks during the war in Syria during June and early July. A third column under Maj R.J. Hardy – Harcol – was despatched to secure Kirkuk.

Meanwhile, whilst this excitement was continuing, 10 Indian Division was moving out of the Basra area up both Tigris and Euphrates rivers to Baghdad. The only hindrance earlier had been lack of suitable transport, but equipment had flooded into the port during previous weeks and much had also been requisitioned from the civilian population. In mid-June the Euphrates Brigade (20 Indian Brigade) reached Habbaniya in only two days' hard travelling by water and road after leaving Ur, and the Tigris Brigade (21 Indian Brigade), less two battalions but comprising 1,400 troops and 210 vehicles, took six days to move from Basra to Kut in requisitioned steamers and hastily converted barges. The operation was appropriately called *Regatta*. The following day command for all of Iraq passed back to GHQ India, responsibility falling to LtGen Quinan, with Slim given command of all of northern Iraq. The impression that both Quinan and Slim were keen to provide was that British forces in Iraq were of considerably greater strength than was in fact the case, reinforcements in the form of 17 and 24 Indian Brigades arriving in Basra on 9 and 16 June respectively. By 18 June the 'occupation' of Iraq was largely complete. Powell's 20 Indian Brigade was in Mosul with a battalion guarding the oilfield at Kirkuk. Slim's headquarters had been established in Baghdad together with a garrison of two infantry battalions and two artillery field regiments. The 2/8 Gurkha Rifles guarded Haditha, Rutbah and Falluja and Weld's 21 Indian Brigade was at Kut.

Both Habforce and 10 Indian Division were now ideally placed to support the British and Free French operation against Vichy Syria, which began on 8 June 1941. That, however, is another story.

CONCLUSION

I n a matter of 30 days the British had, under threat of attack by Iraqi forces at RAF Habbaniya, initiated and won a war that was nevertheless forced on them by a nationalist political clique determined to remove British influence from Iraq and to replace it with that of Germany, at a time when Iraq was critical to Great Britain's survival. That Britain needed to fight to preserve its rights in Iraq was understood clearly by the Prime Minister who saw that to lose control of Iraq would not just deny Britain her precious oil, but allow Germany to dominate the whole of the Middle East, Persian Gulf and Indian Ocean, threaten Palestine and Egypt from the east, cut off the aerial line of communication to India and menace India itself. The loss of Iraq would have made the retention of the Suez Canal impossible, especially if Rommel had managed to force his way in from the west.

These threats, at a time when Germany had yet to commit itself to *Barbarossa*, were very real at the time and justified all the pressure Churchill and the Chiefs of Staff, who unanimously supported the Prime Minister, brought to bear on a reluctant Wavell. Churchill's instinct, mirroring that of both Linlithgow and Auchinleck in India, that a decisive blow against Iraq was necessary despite the paucity of resources available to Wavell for the task, was undoubtedly the correct one.

Three separate factors contributed to the British success in Iraq. The first was the extraordinary defence of Habbaniya by the plucky impudence of the ill-equipped Training School, flying makeshift aircraft with half-trained crews. By taking the initiative into their own hands the gallant aircrew of RAF Habbaniya and the relative handful of infantrymen guarding the wire not only retrieved the strategic initiative in Iraq for Great Britain but also defeated the Iraqi Air Force and demoralized a large part of its army in the process. Sadly, the part played by the RAF forces within Habbaniya was never formally recognized by either honours or awards.

The second was that Auchinleck's determination to build up substantial forces in southern Iraq in April to send a strong signal to Rashid Ali's regime about Britain's intention to defend its interests in the country was finally vindicated by events the following month. The true state of the troop movement into Basra was not appreciated by either Rashid Ali or the Germans, and may well have contributed to the premature collapse of Iraqi resistance. By the end of April the Germans calculated that two Indian Divisions totalling some 28,000 men and 160 warplanes had arrived in Iraq, whereas in actual fact only a single brigade had arrived, bringing with it no transport, tanks or aircraft. The psychological value of the landings vastly outweighed their physical reality.

The third factor was the arrival of Kingcol in Iraq by 18 May, followed by the remainder of Habforce on 25 May. This force, sent at the insistence of London, provided the troops necessary to conduct the land campaign that followed the collapse of Iraqi resistance at Habbaniya. At the end of the fighting at Habbaniya the odds still appeared to be stacked against Britain. Luftwaffe reinforcements were soon to arrive, an Iraqi brigade still guarded the Euphrates crossing at Ramadi and at least one brigade defended Falluja. But Habforce doubled the size of Roberts' forces based at Habbaniya and offered the chance of advancing towards Baghdad in the hope that this brazen opportunism might just be enough to panic the Iraqis into surrender. It was.

Two other factors featured heavily in Great Britain's final victory. The first was the inability of the Iraqi forces to seize the initiative from the British at an early stage of the fighting. Instead, in attempting to use the Habbaniya besiegers as a political tool, Rashid Ali and the Golden Square lost the military initiative as soon as the garrison was able to strike back. Thereafter the Iraqi forces were always on the back foot, despite overwhelmingly superior numbers.

The second lay in the inability of the Germans to exploit the situation in Iraq to their advantage quickly enough. The opportunities open to the Germans had they acted quickly were considerable but they were too busy in Crete between 15 and 31 May and in preparations for *Barbarossa* to give it the attention it required. The *Fliegerführer Irak* was too small and too poorly supported logistically to play a significant role in the campaign and during the last days of fighting Junck's aircraft were grounded due to a lack of spare parts, the need for repairs and the shortage of bombs. Italian aircraft only participated in the final days, and in small numbers.

Both Churchill and Auchinleck were convinced that every risk had to be taken as early as possible to prevent an escalation (leading to armed German intervention in the country), something that Britain would then be unable to control. Rashid Ali's gauntlet had to be accepted, and although the tiny number of troops available to take up the challenge was regrettable, immediate military action was essential, if only to signal Britain's political determination to use military force to resolve the issue in her favour. A firm hand in Iraq was a necessary precursor to any subsequent political action precisely because Rashid Ali, as Auchinleck and Churchill correctly surmised, had no intention of doing anything but overturning the established order, handing over Iraqi oil and resources to Germany, allowing the establishment of strong German military bases across the country for the pursuance of her war aims elsewhere in the region and of removing Great Britain and her influence entirely. If Britain had caved in to Rashid Ali's threats by seeking a negotiated settlement, it would have seriously weakened Britain's standing in the region as a whole, and made it more rather than less difficult for her to deal with Arab nationalist claims in other parts of the Middle East because her reputation for not bowing to violent blackmail would have been fatally compromised. As it was, the military risks paid off, in a brilliant series of victories, each in their own way built largely on bluff and the psychological domination of the enemy, but which firmly secured Great Britain's eastern flank and gave it her first victory of the Second World War.

THE BATTLEFIELD TODAY

At the time of writing, Iraq was not yet ready to provide the security and amenities necessary for the ordinary traveller wishing to visit the sites of the battles of 1941. Travellers from the United Kingdom were advised to consult the Foreign Office (www.fco.gov.uk). Otherwise, it was likely that only members of the security forces would have the opportunity to visit the sites.

Little evidence now remains in Basra and Baghdad of the events described in this book. In Basra, the development of the wharves and the expansion of Basra town itself have long overgrown the relatively small settlements that existed in 1941. However, many of the original buildings remain at RAF Shaibah, home of 244 Squadron, whose Vincents were involved in the battles of 1941 and through which many reinforcements passed.

Tracks have become roads and roads have become dual-lane highways congested with scurrying traffic. Hamlets that were villages in 1941 have, in the main, merged to form villages and towns, and towns have sprouted and grown everywhere, especially along the rivers and major arterial routes. The desert is no longer empty, but with its size still retains the power to surprise. The fleeting presence of the wandering Bedouin is no longer as apparent as it was in 1941 and the Marsh Arabs, who for centuries made their precarious living amongst the Tigris waterways and marshlands, have long been swept by Ba'ath Party totalitarianism into the dustbin of history.

The main exception is RAF Habbaniya which, whilst untidy and overgrown, retains much evidence of its previous existence. The air field and cantonment were used by the RAF until 1959, and thereafter by the Iraqi Air Force, and much of the original infrastructure was retained and has survived through to the present. The tree-lined avenues still stand proudly, although the rose beds have long given way to weeds, roofs sag under the weight of the years and paint is a distant memory. The RAF Habbaniya cemetery is in a very poor state but the 289 graves (including those who died in the events in 1941) appear to be intact and coalition forces are attempting some restoration. Abandoned vehicles, aircraft and artillery pieces from the RAF era are dotted about. In 2005 the civil part of the cantonment became home to refugees displaced by counter-insurgency operations in nearby Falluja.

At Falluja itself, whilst the town has grown substantially since 1941, the old iron bridge remains unchanged from the war, and would be instantly recognizable to any veteran of the fighting there in May 1941. In April 2004 it gained notoriety as the site of an atrocity against civilian American contractors.

An active veteran's organization exists in the United Kingdom to perpetuate the memory of the air base and all those who served in Iraq at

RAF Habbaniya, RAF Shaibah and RAF Basra over the decades before the British withdrawal from Iraq, as well as members of the coalition forces with recent service in Iraq. This is run by Dr Christopher Morris who can be contacted at RAF.Habbaniya@btinternet.com. The website, which has links to other related organizations, can be found at www.habbaniya.org. It carries a number of recent photographs of the Habbaniya site. Additionally, a website commemorating the work of the Iraq Levies has been established by Gaby Kiwarkis at www.gabylevies.freeservers.com. This, too, has links to other related websites across the internet

BIBLIOGRAPHY

Buckley, Christopher, *Five Ventures: Iraq–Syria–Persia–Madagascar–Dodecanese,* HMSO, London (1954)

Churchill, Winston, *The Second World War, Volume 3: The Grand Alliance*, Cassell, London (1950)

Connell, John, *Wavell: Scholar and Soldier, To June 1941*, Harcourt, New York (1964)

Dudgeon, Anthony, *Hidden Victory: The Battle of Habbaniya, May 1941*, Tempus, Stroud (2000)

de Chair, Somerset, *The Golden Carpet*, Faber & Faber, London (1944)

Glubb, John, *The Story of the Arab Legion*, Hodder & Stoughton, London (1948)

Lyman, Robert, *A Close-Run Thing: The Struggle for Mastery in the Middle East, 1941*, Constable & Robinson, London (2006)

Masters, John, *The Road Past Mandalay*, Michael Joseph, London (1961)

Pal, Dharm, *Official History of Indian Armed Forces in the Second World War. The Campaign in Western Asia*, Combined Inter-Services Historical Section, Delhi (1957)

Playfair, I.S.O., *History of the Second World War. The Mediterranean and Middle East, Volume 2: The Germans Come to the Help of Their Ally, 1941*, HMSO, London (1956)

Raugh, Harold, *Wavell in the Middle East, 1939-1941: A Study in Generalship,* Brassey's, London (1993)

Shores, Christopher, *Dust Clouds in the Middle East*, Grub Street, London (1996)

Stark, Freya, *East is West*, John Murray, London (1945)

Warner, Geoffrey, *Politics and Strategy of the Second World War. Iraq and Syria, 1941*, Davis-Poynter, London (1974)

INDEX